STORY

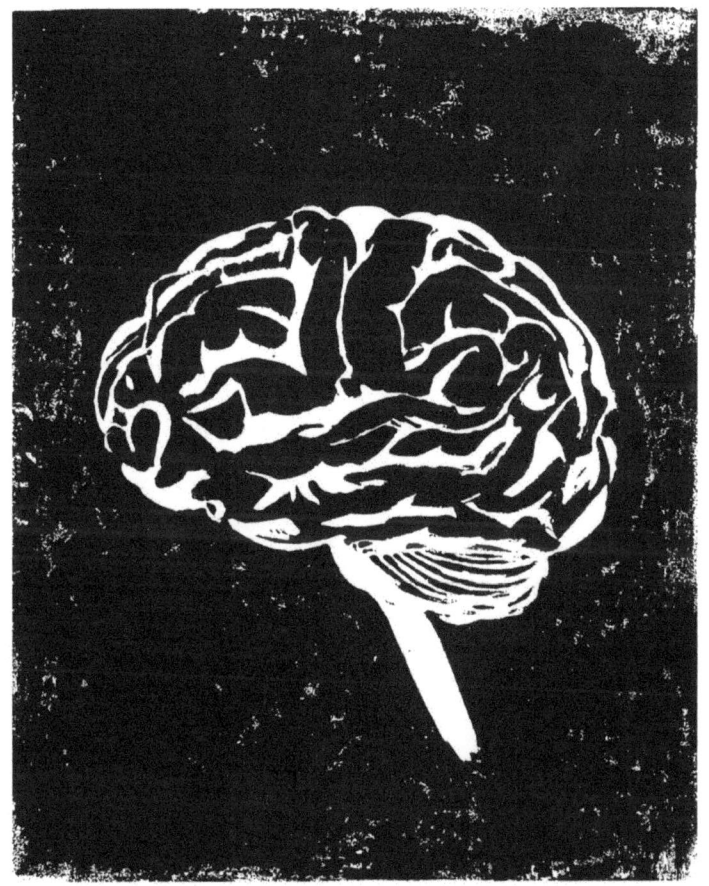

THE CURRENCY OF INFLUENCE

JON TIMOTHY NEWSOME

STORY
THE CURRENCY OF INFLUENCE

Copyright © 2025 by Jon Timothy Newsome

All rights reserved. No part of this publication may be reproduced, stored in a retrieval system, or transmitted, in any form or by any means, except as may be expressly permitted by the 1976 Copyright Act or by Jon Timothy Newsome in writing.

ISBN: 979-8-218-61867-4 (paperback)

Whilst every effort has been made to ensure that the information contained within this book is correct at the time of going to press, the author and publisher can take no responsibility for the errors or omissions contained within.

NeuroStory Press
www.storycurrency.com
www.neuroscienceofpersuasion.com

Cover: Designed by Engela de Beer

Book design by Wordzworth

To my wife, Michele, thank you for tolerating my endless—
and sometimes failed—attempts to distill the complex into
something meaningful. Your patience, even when you were
only pretending to be interested, means the world to me.
And to my children, Jordan, Emerson, and Sylvia, who are still
scratching their heads, wondering "Why is dad writing a book?"—
I don't have an answer that will satisfy you, but here we are.

Contents

Preface — vii

Prologue: The Era of Story — xiii

1. Your World Today
   Your Deal or Opportunity Is Better Than Your Deck — 1

2. Everybody's a Storyteller, eh?
   Academic, Personal, and Business Stories — 7

3. Aristotle Meets (Rocket) Science
   Building Your Persuasion Foundation — 17

4. Being the Tortoise in Aesop's Fable (Not the Hare)
   Proving Stories Didn't Require a DNA Super Gene — 23

5. Your Brain's Factory Settings
   Understanding Audience Science — 29

6. Your Audience Is Not a Hard Drive
   Cognitive Load — 39

7. Emotion Is the Potion
   Your Audience Is Why You're There — 51

8. The Audience Whisperer
   Uncomplicating Your Audience — 59

9. Pure Message Moonshine
   Distilling Content to Meaning — 69

10. The Science of Story
    EQ Primacy — 95

11. The *EQ Sandwich*™ — 105

12. Threading Your Story Together
    The Secret Sauce Is Red Thread — 115

13. Following Our Own Recipe
    Guess How This Book Is Structured … — 133

14. Winning Your World
    Synthesize Story — 137

15. Your World Tomorrow
    The Currency of Success — 143

Acknowledgments — 147

Preface

Who on earth would ever create a job description requiring the review of over 1 million presentation slides and critiquing slide messaging until your eyes bleed? While it's been exaggerated, truly no one has died from death by bullet points ... though I'm still gathering data on that as I am routinely surprised by how horrific presentations can be. In medieval times, people might have considered this profession a more effective torture mechanism than a career choice, right up there with death by a thousand paper cuts. Yet without this torture, I would never have realized just how desperately the business world needs a story.

After nearly two decades of serving close to 800 customers, including high-profile global enterprises, the requests to write this book came from countless leaders and road warriors who recognized the need for these insights to be scaled and shared. They knew there had to be a better way to present high-value messages to mission-critical audiences, and they wanted others to benefit from it too.

Yet, as funny as it seems to me, here I am championing the art (and science) of storytelling for nearly two decades, and it took me this long to pen my story about stories! While the idea of writing a book has been ever-present, dangled before me by eager publishers and well-meaning peers, my unwavering commitment to my clients and continually evolving and proving our story model always took precedence over the authorship of a book. But the scales tipped as I ventured onto stages and into corporate sanctums speaking about storytelling.

Story: The Currency of Influence

My target shifted to introduce, on a grander scale, the high-stakes dealmaker to the genuine value of storytelling—the sound foundational mechanisms through the *Neuroscience of Persuasion*[SM], that enable efficient story construction, not just quick fixes. I won't sugarcoat this: Mastering storytelling, the modern currency of influence, is a learned discipline that comes through intensive practice.

Growing up a highly competitive kid from the Midwest, I had wild dreams of becoming an astronaut, a professional golfer, and even a race car driver. By the time I hit fifth grade, I took a job one summer delivering papers without ever thinking about the consequences of that job in the winter. But there I was with a giant bag of newspapers slung over my shoulder, navigating snow- and ice-covered sidewalks on my green Schwinn bike. As challenging as those freezing cold post-school afternoons were, I relished the entrepreneurial responsibilities—managing money and meeting obligations. A few years later, realizing my schoolmates had a serious sweet tooth, I expanded to buying and reselling donuts and pastries at a 100% markup from a shop I passed on the way to school. Not quite the space race I had dreamed of, but it was my little peek into a future that awaited me. My parents' insistence that I earn my own spending money shaped my approach to business, even if I never made it to the moon or the PGA Tour.

After college, I would have never predicted that I'd end up running a storytelling agency—a concept that I couldn't have even defined back then. But today, I'm thrilled to be in this position, and here's a family tidbit that accentuates the idea: As I sat one day with a five-year-old, my wide-eyed great nephew, I disclosed my job is about spinning tales. He's convinced I've hit the jackpot. Frankly, I can't disagree. No communications degree hangs on my wall, and while I'm not an educated scientist, I've been fortunate to collaborate with brilliant team members shaping the *Neuroscience of Persuasion*[SM]. Perhaps the closest I've veered toward professional storytelling was my stint as a *Dale Carnegie*[TM] instructor, teaching what they dubbed a "communications course." And yes, while I've left dreams of the racetracks and golf courses for boardrooms and stages, there's still a bit of that speed-loving Midwestern kid in me, especially when I'm driving to a golf course.

During a pitch in the early 2000s, I first realized that the structure of a story mattered. After 18 years of working for others and reporting to a board of directors, I found myself in a position where I possessed the rights to a utility patent from my former employer. Together, with a colleague, we faced the challenge of unlocking its value for us and for potential stakeholders. It was one of life's seminal moments where I realized I had a monetizable idea. Once we had perfected the engineering, we faced an even bigger challenge: how to tell its story so that we could convince the rest of the world. This is a common trap—leaders invest countless months perfecting their innovation but just days preparing how to present it. Great ideas deserve great stories. For reasons even I can't pin down, I've always been obsessed with business presentations and have consistently sought ways to expound on optimal differentiation.

In Augusta, Georgia, close to my home in Atlanta, my colleague and I found ourselves in one of those rare pivotal career meetings, pitching a product based on an innovative utility patent to a Fortune 500 company. Instead of leaning heavily on visual aids, that were crafted by an external creative service, we chose a different path. Sure, we had jazzy-looking materials, but the pitch strategy centered on expressing a deep understanding of the company's supply-chain complexities and the emotional consequences. This was a deliberate shift away from merely presenting an innovative product. The entire pitch would take less than 15 minutes, but the meeting enthusiastically lasted several hours.

The aftermath of that meeting proved to be nothing short of life altering. Our pitch, which lasted a mere 15 minutes—admittedly a rare unicorn sighting in the corporate world—not only succeeded but also paved the way for a cascade of subsequent meetings. To be clear, this 15-minute pitch took immense work for the distillation into an interesting narrative. The power of that story earned us those subsequent meetings—it wasn't gifted to us. **Great ideas die without great stories. Your narrative deserves as much focus as your solution.** These efforts eventually snowballed into the grand achievement of our utility patent application being notched in the "registered" column, coupled with a licensing deal inked with a Fortune 500 behemoth.

> **Great ideas die without great stories. Your narrative deserves as much focus as your solution.**

For a stretch of years, we basked in the glory of receiving royalties, a perk I believed was only reserved for the likes of rock stars and divas. And if you have ever heard me sing a hymn in a church pew, you'd know singing is not my path to earning riches. However, although the economic boost was nice, the true game changer wasn't the influx of cash—it was that pivotal meeting.

During that fast 15-minute presentation, we spent a disproportionate 11 minutes dissecting the intricate woes of their manufacturing and supply-chain logistics. By delving into their nitty-gritty situations, we made the impending solution feel inevitable. If we knew their business inside out, then we must have possessed a solution so enticing it practically sparkled. Yet in today's business landscape, where technological complexities crash over us like a tsunami, there's a tendency to have your solution outpace the fundamental simplicity of the problem at hand. Ask yourself if your company, service, or product today is placing more value on your solution than their situation.

Pitching for a mere 15 minutes not only piqued their interest but triggered a parade of requests like, "Would you mind walking through this again with more of our gang?" "Mind running through it one more time with our senior vice president of really important stuff?" What happened next still amazes me—and shows exactly what's possible when you get this right: Never in this meeting nor in 30 years of deal opportunities have I witnessed a prospective client exude more acceptance to a presentation pitch with so little care as to the details of our innovative product. This wasn't about having the perfect product; it was about having the perfect story. And here's the good news: While you can't always control your product's features, you can always control how you present them. They were all in, hook, line, and sinker. This level of engagement isn't a matter of luck—it's a matter of method, and it's exactly what you're about to learn.

The brevity of the pitch was certainly in our favor. It was a tiny David's slingshot against the Goliath of dull, exceedingly verbose business presentations that seem to dominate the corporate landscape. In hindsight, as I revisited that moment in my mind's eye, it became abundantly clear that our success hinged less on extolling the virtues of our unbelievably brilliant and innovative product and more on aligning ourselves with demonstrating our knowledge of the client's unique circumstances in their challenging environments. Little did I know this epiphany would launch me on a 5-year journey orbiting the realm of how to structure better stories in the business environment. This voyage eventually gave birth in 2014 to what I now proudly call the *Neuroscience of Persuasion*^{SM}, a highly digestible framework for making waves in the world of influence.

Now, suppose you've picked up this book with the noble intention of refining your presentation skills solely to impress your audience with your offering. In that case, you might be missing the grand point of becoming an astronaut without realizing you first need to be a pilot. Let's rewind to that pivotal meeting scenario I mentioned earlier. Our goal wasn't just to impress them; we were aiming squarely for their minds to be persuaded.

Time to pump those carbon-fiber racing brakes. Before we sprint ahead to the world of persuasion, let's understand what's really at stake here. Back in 2009, Warren Buffett told Columbia University students that "Learning public speaking will improve your worth by 50%." But in today's content-saturated world, where technology has amplified every voice while paradoxically making genuine connection rarer, that 50% represents a conservative estimate. When everyone else is avoiding

Story: The Currency of Influence

the spotlight, mastering storytelling isn't just an advantage—it's your fast track to pulling away from the pack.

In today's world of effortless access to the internet, everyone's expected to whip up a presentation for themselves or the boss. Whether you signed up for the presentation circus, you're a presenter in this digital age. Presenting has transcended into the shiny new currency of success. This is exactly what Warren Buffet was envisioning over a decade ago, but today, it's juiced with steroids. Knowing your product or service like a champ gets you on the starting grid of the race. Articulating a good story is how we get to the podium for the trophy celebration. So, here's the million-dollar question: Who can tell the best story?

Prologue:
The Era of Story

Imagine you're about to present an opportunity for a megadeal. Are you going to win? Crush that presentation? Are you walking out of that room with that big smile on your face because you know your competition doesn't have your influential finesse to move the prospect the way you do?

You may have closed large deals, raised capital, been a part of business-development-winning teams, yet does thinking of yourself as a consistent deal-winner with persuasive prowess seem like a stretch? Consider this: People who changed the world, their industry, or community articulated ideas through better storytelling. I am inspired by the likes of monumental business stories from Gates, Welch, Musk, and Schulz, and how their ability to focus on a captivating story created and moved markets. Flashback to 2007: Steve Jobs unveils a product—the *iPhone*^{TM}—reshaping billions of lives. Yet, it wasn't just about the device, but how he delivered the message. Jobs wasn't just talking; he was storytelling. For the leadership at Apple, it was more than selling a value proposition with benefits. They understood that realizing how important the skill set of story development and sharing it in a memorable fashion can elevate a career, a company, and even a market.

Still having trouble envisioning yourself as the next industry icon through your storytelling skills? Fair enough, since being at the

Story: The Currency of Influence

pinnacle of your discipline like Steve Jobs, or becoming an Olympic champion isn't your goal? Understandable. But how might training like a champion for a month transform your fitness? Might that be enough to win the next two megadeals? Fifteen chapters are all you'll need. This book offers science-researched mechanisms that not only guide you into how to execute stories but keep the *why* front and center.

Meanwhile, your competition is taking shortcuts. They think they've discovered a hack. While you're reading this book, they think they're getting a leg up as they type *storytelling tips* into a search engine, and boom—the bombardment begins: the two techniques, 3 C's, 4 P's, 5 traits, 6 rules.... Overwhelming? Certainly, but now we have the competition exactly where we want them. Looking and sounding like everybody else, rather than focusing on a narrative between humans. If storytelling was a 3-minute article read from the internet, if mastering business storytelling was as easy as reading an online article, every LinkedIn influencer would close billion-dollar deals. Save the internet of tips and tricks for your competitors. While they're busy memorizing buzzwords, you'll be crafting narratives that resonate in C-suites long after the *PowerPoint*™ clicks off.

Merely telling a story is not the secret for winning deals and raising gobs of capital, in the same way that technology is not the secret of digital transformation. The secret is understanding how to develop a story that is relevant to your audience.

Storytelling is more than just a mere technique compiled on presentation slides; it's the currency of influence. The sooner you let go of conventional approaches and give your opportunity the story it deserves, the closer you will be to raising that gob of capital or winning the deal. John Medina, a molecular biologist and author of *Brain Rules*, puts it bluntly: "Please, do two things: (1) Burn your current PowerPoint presentations. (2) Make new ones." His directive isn't just provocative—it's necessary. Starting fresh allows you to cut through the cognitive overload that modern technology often imposes and

Prologue: The Era of Story

to build something worthy of your opportunity. Today, whether we acknowledge it, we're all storytellers.

Thousands of CEOs have developed worthy ideas associated with megatrends. Still, their firms wallow in mediocrity, failing to punch through the stratosphere that they believe is rightly theirs. The mistake? Delegating storytelling to teams who rely on quick-fix solutions from the internet to win over high-value clients. Without a deep understanding of storytelling principles, these businesses remain mediocre, unable to win high-value clients or navigate transformational changes.

Storytelling isn't just another fleeting buzzword, like business process reengineering or big data, which came and went as transient corporate jargon. No, storytelling boasts ancient roots, which we'll delve into later. Anything that has endured millennia isn't merely trendy. As modern society spirals into technological complexities, there's an urgent need to cut through the noise, simplify, and humanize your next big deal opportunity. That's where the age-old art of storytelling reclaims its vital role. Inside the corridors of the corporate world we have seen *story* thrown around like the flavor-of-the-month buzzword, except it's not going away because it's always been there. Today, we are just illuminating *story*'s importance, desperately needed as a forward-thinking tool to make sense of a more technology-driven, complex, and chaotic world. If you are content to just survive, keep pretending it's a trendy term. Courtesy of Vilfredo Pareto, his 80/20 principle rarely fails; 20% will do something with this information. As for the rest, you might as well use this manual to beef up your bookshelf and give off an air of story knowledge without doing the heavy lifting.

But know this, 80% of the tools you need to become a story master are right here in front of you. And the other 20% will come from putting these mechanisms into play and learning from those experiences. Master this skill and you'll outperform your peers. For those business development teams that are interested in capturing the megadeal, and those entrepreneurs who need to raise gobs of capital (yes, I said gobs) to fund their market-busting ideas, welcome to the era of story.

1

Your World Today

Your Deal or Opportunity Is Better Than Your Deck

The 3-Minute Trap

Your next deal opportunity is around the corner. While your competition skims 3-minute articles on storytelling, you want to crush it with something more substantial. You think storytelling might be the differentiator. But the value of business storytelling isn't in clever analogies. It's in your audience discovering relevance for them and how they can retell it. When your story connects, the audience couldn't care less about the slides, because they can tell your story in their own words. I call this verbal passing of the torch "on-communication" (a term a friend of mine coined after one too many glasses of wine)—where your story travels strictly through speech, living on in hallway conversations or boardroom discussions, not just shared files. While you can share a document, video, or presentation, the essence of a story lies in its ability to be conveyed from person to person through speech.

From Sharing to "Verbally On-Communicating"

It is in these moments of verbal transmission that you, as a dealmaker, realize the power of a compelling narrative. It transforms from a mere collection of clever phrases to something potent and memorable that new clients can understand and retell in their own words. Consider this: most high-stakes deal meetings conclude with stakeholders struggling to summarize or retell the pitch they've just heard. But when your story resonates so clearly that your prospect can effortlessly recount it to their colleagues, you've achieved something extraordinary. Your narrative must be verbally on-communicated through the leadership corridors of the prospect's organization. **When your story travels through leadership corridors without you, you've separated yourself from the competition.** When that happens, you win.

> **When your story travels through leadership corridors without you, you've separated yourself from the competition.**

The Aesop Standard

Imagine you must convey the value of a prudent, patient strategy to win. How would you approach it? Most business leaders would reach for their tool kit—perhaps a 3-part webinar series or a *PowerPoint*™ deck hastily loaded with jargon and flashy graphics.

This half-baked effort is the business norm. It pales in stark contrast to the sheer brilliance of Aesop's fable, "The Tortoise and the Hare." In mere sentences, Aesop crafted a narrative so profound, yet straightforward, that it has echoed through millennia. There's no fluff, just a memorable lesson: Slow and steady wins the race. While our modern tales often get lost in translation or forgotten by the next quarterly report, Aesop's wisdom remains as clear and resonant as ever—surviving for 18 centuries before the invention of the printing press. There will be more on our friend Aesop later in this book. For now, concerning that deal opportunity that's just around the corner, ask yourself if your message, narrative, or content is articulated and differentiated well enough to outlast your business meeting. If not, keep reading.

Win Big, Lose Big

Modern college athletics continues to shatter records, not just in championship victories but in billion-dollar deal failures. I've witnessed these epic financial fumbles with more than casual interest. Throughout my life various family members have competed at the collegiate level, so college sports have been a constant thread over dinner. The stark reality emerging from these failures teaches us something crucial to modern business. Even the biggest deals collapse when leaders fail to tell the right story.

The need for powerful storytelling surfaces everywhere in business today, but nowhere more dramatically than in collegiate athletic conferences. Here, the landscape has been volatile, with contractions and expansions. Megadeal television contracts seem to be the goal to bring financial stability to their member universities. I suspect that for the conferences that have lost out, messaging got stripped down to mere fundamental economics. This is something Nobel Prize winner Daniel Kahneman proved is detrimental and that we will shed light on in later chapters. In this scenario, a conference focusing on viewer metrics and media deals created a blind spot—the inevitable consolidation, because of football, into super conferences. If your story framing is all about the metrics, you've missed what truly drives decisions: **Algorithms don't make decisions; humans do.** The real story wasn't in the spreadsheets, it was in the fans, athletic administrators, and head coaches all wanting a simpler path to crowning champions. Understanding these human stakeholders should have fundamentally reshaped how those metrics and economics were positioned in the first place.

> **Algorithms don't make decisions; humans do.**

Your Algorithm or Your Voice?

Boil your argument down to just economics and the facts without the underpinning of contextual storytelling, and you're mortgaging a future without ownership. Think about that metaphor for a moment. When you rely solely on data and analytics to make your case, you're essentially taking out a high-interest loan on your audience's attention. The data-minded executive will argue that they will follow your logic, and I agree, they will. But this following will be temporary. Because without story context, without a human connection, that attention becomes a debt you can never fully repay. The numbers might raise an eyebrow, but they won't give you lasting influence in the corridors where leaders make decisions.

Your competitors are doing this right now—dumping data, spewing specs, and wondering why their brilliant analytics aren't closing deals. They're accumulating presentation debt, sliding deeper underwater with every bullet point, drowning in their own expertise while their audiences drift away, hoping that the next presentation opportunity that they must sit through has a group of presenters that understands what they really desire—human connection and relevance to their world.

So, if you are thirsty enough to not lose the deal, recognize that your deal deserves a story as interesting as its opportunity. When your deck matches the power of your deal, when your narrative equals your value solution, you're not just presenting—you're building equity in every conversation, every pitch, every meeting. That's not just owning the room; that's owning your future today.

2

Everybody's a Storyteller, eh?

Academic, Personal, and Business Stories

The Definition of Storytelling

I've heard hundreds, if not thousands, of business executives shamelessly refer to their content as a *story,* and I cringed every time. Business development presentations, RFP documents, and brochures that are verbose are nothing more than an information dump and likely die a quick death within 24 to 48 hours after delivery. Let us be careful what we call a story.

A foundational definition of storytelling is necessary before discussing how to craft and tell the best story. Given my childhood dreams of mastering the greens as a professional golfer (among other ambitious pursuits), it feels fitting to say before we tee off into the expansive fairway of this discussion, let's make sure we're all aiming for the same hole: a clear definition of storytelling. And no, I don't mean those internet gems that define it as "a collection of ideas to be expressed, sometimes theatrically." We need a strong, precise, and clear definition that focuses on the relevancy of our audience.

/ˈstôrēˌteliNG/

Storytelling is a uniquely human practice of triggering emotions through language, allowing us to learn the lessons we need to survive and thrive without experiencing them firsthand.

1 of 4—Storytelling is a uniquely human practice ...

The first half a dozen words are straightforward; it's a *human practice*. At least, as far as we can tell, animals and plants cannot engage in storytelling. Artificial intelligence is attempting to mimic humans in this arena, but it will require deep methodology and a reservoir of accurate and compelling examples to make a story sound like a human and not like AI trying to sound like a human.

2 of 4 ... of triggering emotions through language, ...

Now, interpreting the next few words, let us buckle up and navigate the 21-turn racetrack ahead: *triggering emotions*. This is where the new race car driver is side by side with another car heading into a turn and grips the wheel tighter and brakes early. Similarly, business leaders often hesitate when steering into emotional narratives. But science already confirms what master storytellers already know—that stories in business settings affect us physically. Things like heart rate variability (HRV), brain activity, areas such as the temporal cortices, and right amygdala[1] register effects from storytelling. Phew! That was a mouthful of brainy words to prove that we can measure and *trigger emotions through language*.

3 of 4 ... allowing us to learn the lessons we need ...

The most critical words in the definition of storytelling—*learn the lessons*—are also the most ambiguous. Stories driving business success

---

[1] Wallentin, M., A. H. Nielson, P. Vuust, A. Dohn, A. Roepstorff, and T. E. Lund, "Amygdala and Heart Rate Variability Responses from Listening to Emotionally Intense Parts of a Story," *NeuroImage* 58, no. 3 (2011): 963–973, DOI: 10.1016/j.neuroimage.2011.06.077.

must impart lasting knowledge, not just temporary understanding. **Stories are not meant to be forgotten—they should live through others who retell them.** Learning and remembering are key attributes of a story, and without them working in harmony, your story becomes like a race car that's lost contact with its team of race strategists, overtaken by more-focused competitors. Are your pitch documents getting lapped? Let's reconnect with the strategy team on the pit wall and learn how to win this race.

> **Stories are not meant to be forgotten—they should live through others who retell them.**

Science points to the most efficient practice in engaging our audience to *learn the lessons* we present. To grasp the essence, it's crucial to understand a sequential progression backed by science[2]. You first need to capture their attention using what experts call *multisensory enhancement*. **Storytelling isn't just about words—it's about creating an experience through sights, sounds, and even atmosphere.** Think of a race car driver focused on their acceleration exit point through a turn while simultaneously being acutely aware of an unusual sound emanating from their engine compartment. They're processing both visual and auditory cues to make quick decisions, just like your audience does when processing your message.

> **Storytelling isn't just about words—it's about creating an experience through sights, sounds, and even atmosphere.**

Second, once you captivate the audience, the narrative's focus shifts to maintaining attention, along with triggering emotions. Research

---

[2] Lunn, J., A. Sjoblom, J. Ward, S. Soto-Faraco, and S. Forster, "Multisensory Enhancement of Attention Depends on Whether You Are Already Paying Attention," *Cognition* 187 (2019): 38–49. DOI: 10.1016/j.cognition.2019.02.008.

underscores the vital role of attention in processing multisensory stimuli. Effective storytelling that evokes emotions not only captures the audience's attention but also renders the message more memorable and impactful. Using emotional narratives in storytelling can effectively engage the audience initially and equip them to remember your ideas for sharing with others.

In today's world, the term storytelling has become a corporate sound bite. But for business leaders seeking real results, the challenge goes deeper: Just like the race car driver, who navigates sensory cues and emotional focus, we too must craft narratives that resonate emotionally while maintaining our audience's focus. This next section doesn't cater to those interested in academic or entertainment types of storytelling. However, exploring these types briefly provides noteworthy insight into the larger framework to understand stories better.

Storytelling in Academia

Academia tells stories through well-conceived research papers and articles, aiming to persuade through structured arguments. Yet most postgraduate work cannot reach beyond its specialized audience. The writing is often so dense that readers can't summarize it verbally days later. If you haven't learned the lesson well enough and can't recall it after a few days, then it's not working.

The challenge of all writing, especially academic writing, is that it can sometimes miss the mark because of the underlying process. Professor Larry McEnerney, who led a writing program at the University of Chicago, once remarked, "Students write papers in academia for teachers who are paid to care about the students."[3] This highlights the issue: Outside of academia, readers are neither obligated

---

3 UChicago Social Sciences, "Leadership Lab: The Craft of Writing Effectively," posted June 2014, YouTube, https://youtu.be/vtIzMaLkCaM?si=XXyCF5BqE_Do7DXr.

nor incentivized to wrestle with complex content. From my experience as a postgraduate theology student, I've seen how even family members, interested in theological insights, shy away from my dense and intricate essays. Like most people, they avoid texts that feel like academic doorstops, which illustrates how an academic style of writing can often miss the broader audience by not considering how unmotivated readers engage with the material.

Storytelling in Personal Entertainment

In the previous section on academic storytelling, we hinted at the perspective of how a writer or content developer operates on a completely different axis from how a person reads. This intersection between the two parties can be quite small. If you've read a white paper lately, you'll instantly understand the communicative challenges between writer and reader. However, within the practice of "personal storytelling," there is a far more significant awareness related to the needs of the audience.

The Prisoner's Apprentice, a put-you-on-the-edge-of-your-seat story by novelist Cheyenne Richards, exemplifies a novel that rivetingly grabs the reader from the start: "By the Fourth of July, everyone with a boat was out on Cayuga Lake, dragging chains and hooks and fishing nets, looking for bodies."

What the author realizes is how intimate of a tango exists between the writer and reader. The reader's mind fills in all the details based on their unique experiences and memories, creating a deeply personal dance of interpretation. Biologically, this happens because the cortices in our brains are adept at filling in gaps in our perception. When we read the novel author's words about *boats on a lake dragging nets*, our brains compile these elements into short, movie-like flashes, drawing from similar scenes we've witnessed or elements we can piece together. That's why your version of a lake being dragged for bodies on the Fourth of July will never be the same as mine, and neither will match the author, Cheyenne Richards. No two brains interpret or store information in the same way. And therein lies the magic—each person's brain makes the story uniquely relevant, but only if you, the communicator or dealmaker, know how to lead this delicate tango. That's exactly what this book will teach you.

Movies add visual details, but the best ones allow the viewer to fill in the details between the scenes, cuts, and lines of dialogue. One of the most successful movies in the last half of the twentieth century was Steven Spielberg's *Jaws*®, based on Peter Benchley's book[4]. Through the incidental failure of the mechanical shark, the young director had to improvise with the help of a creative film editor and sound director who were up for the challenge. Collectively, they realized that there was more suspense by letting the viewer fill in the details in their own mind of a shark swimming toward a pair of submerged dangling human legs to the din of ... *dun-DUN, dun-DUN!*

4 of 4 ... *to survive and thrive without experiencing them firsthand*

Having developed a formal definition of storytelling and explored each component over several small sections, we now complete our definition in this section on personal storytelling. This allows us to fully articulate the essence of the phrase: *to survive and thrive without experiencing them firsthand*. Consider a group of moviegoers who have watched the film *Snakes on a Plane*®.[5] While some may argue the film is for escapism or peculiar entertainment, they might be partially correct. On the conscious level, viewers might have wanted a distraction to keep

---

[4] Benchley, Peter, *Jaws*, Bantam, 1975.
[5] *Snakes on a Plane*, directed by David R. Ellis, performances by Samuel L. Jackson, Julianna Margulies, New Line Cinema, 2006.

themselves from thinking about their company's balance sheet. But at a deeper level, it's to learn the lessons they need to survive and thrive in an unforeseen circumstance. The novelist Cheyenne Richards puts it this way; "Underlying every Hollywood trailer and bestseller premise is someone who is nudging the reader or viewers to think, *If we were ever in a situation like this, what would we do?* And then giving them an opportunity to try on that situation risk-free, without their actual job, marriage, or life on the line." Thus, if you ever found yourself in this dastardly situation of poisonous snakes released by a criminal at 32,000 feet, you'd know how to handle this situation, and you'd be ready.

Storytelling in Business

Business leaders now champion storytelling as their secret weapon, especially as they wrestle with explaining increasingly complex technology. Yet here's the irony: While everyone talks about storytelling, most corporate attempts at it barely scratch the surface. Worse still, these superficial approaches get endlessly recycled across the internet, creating an echo chamber of shallow tips and tricks. I know this trap well—I even helped spread one of these popular myths in my storytelling agency's early days: the claim that humans now have attention spans shorter than goldfish.

This was my wake-up call. Here I was, a storytelling expert, caught in the same trap I now warn others about—reaching for quick, catchy statistics instead of doing the deep work. It wasn't until we developed the *Neuroscience of Persuasion*[SM] that we uncovered how far off base that goldfish claim really was. While it's true, that humans get distracted easily, and good storytelling can help capture attention, that 8-second goldfish comparison keeps swimming around (even in popular streaming shows about American football coaches in UK soccer) despite being pure fiction. Science has never proven a goldfish's attention span—how could it? But this perfectly illustrates our problem: We're so hungry for quick solutions to complex challenges we'll bite at any convenient statistic that seems to explain human behavior. The real story about attention and engagement runs much deeper.

Picture this: Business audiences are swimming in distractions, both internal and external, especially in fast-paced environments. Now, throw in what Professor McEnerney stipulated that we highlighted in the earlier academic storytelling section: Presentation authors often structure their content based on their own thinking processes, which does not align with how the audience absorbs information[6] (we'll dive deeper into the science behind this later). The result? Countless ideas, worth millions or even billions of dollars, sailing past the dartboard and sticking uselessly in the wall. **Storytelling has emerged as the quintessential currency of modern success, yet amidst this narrative renaissance, failure awaits those who leave their stories untold.**

Blending the Threads

Let's dissect the three realms of storytelling: academic, personal, and business. Among them, there's one glaring denominator, bar none, that reigns supreme—your audience. While novelists and filmmakers excel at entertainment, and students struggle with academic essays, our focus is on the business reader, the entrepreneur, and the dealmaker. Though these storytelling principles work elsewhere (I've accidentally tested them in family debates with surprising success), business storytelling drove the development of this framework.

After 17 years in business, I went looking for storytelling experts

---

6   UChicago Social Sciences, "Leadership Lab: The Craft of Writing Effectively," YouTube, posted June 2014. https://youtu.be/vtIzMaLkCaM?si=XXyCF5BqE_Do7DXr.

to learn from. Finding none, I had the audacity to start a storytelling agency. That was 18 years ago, and I've watched the demand skyrocket since. Today, we're in the era of storytelling, where the story is the currency of business success. With audiences more informed and harder to impress than ever, the question remains, who can tell the best story?

3

Aristotle Meets (Rocket) Science

Building Your
Persuasion Foundation

Story: The Currency of Influence

Figure 3.1: The four cornerstones of the *Neuroscience of Persuasion*[SM].

There's a Reason They're Called Cornerstones

Dating back to ancient times, the cornerstone was the first stone laid by builders in masonry construction. Both literally and metaphorically, it was the most important stone that set everything in place. The entire integrity of the structure depends on it. Which is why the *Neuroscience of Persuasion*[SM] foundationally begins here. We want you to possess a solid foundation for persuasive storytelling if you're going to rock that next deal.

Arguments built solely on facts and logic—what we'll call "IQ" in this chapter—often fail to persuade. Aristotle discovered this while grinding through 20 years at Plato's Academy, the ancient world's version of philosophical boot camp. Through pure observation and critical reasoning, he discovered what modern scientists would later prove, that **our brains resist action when logic stands alone.**

Aristotle Meets (Rocket) Science

Creating convincing arguments can seem like magic, especially in high-stakes business deals. When faced with weaving together cultural nuances, economic realities, shareholder demands, and power dynamics into a magical story, even seasoned dealmakers can feel overwhelmed. Yet beneath this complexity lies a core foundation. The *Gemini* and *Apollo* missions and dreams inspired one of my earliest childhood ambitions of becoming an astronaut. The awe-inspiring Saturn V rocket, which carried astronauts to the moon and back, fueled this ambition. I promise more on that later.

> **Our brains resist action when logic stands alone.**

We've all heard the saying, "it's not rocket science," which underscores the ironic complexity of rockets. The Saturn V—the rocket that launched humans to the moon—had over 3 million parts and weighed over 6 million pounds (with fuel) at launch. That is the equivalent in weight of 30 blue whales. This complexity of weight and parts requires some serious ingenuity, perhaps even some pixie dust, just to lift off the launch pad. Yet, like most things, there is a foundational simplicity to any rocket ship:

Breaking Down the Complexity of Rocket Science

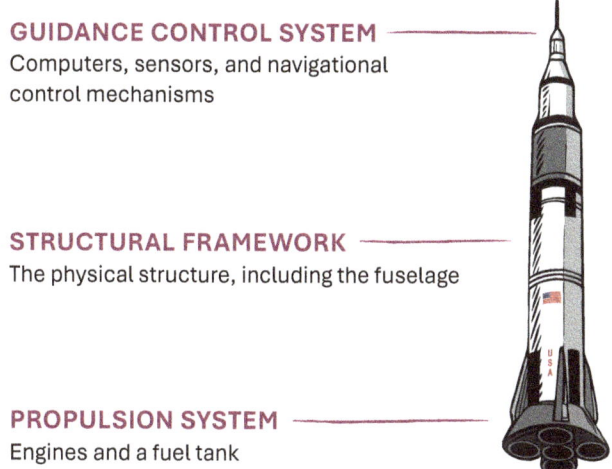

GUIDANCE CONTROL SYSTEM
Computers, sensors, and navigational control mechanisms

STRUCTURAL FRAMEWORK
The physical structure, including the fuselage

PROPULSION SYSTEM
Engines and a fuel tank

Story: The Currency of Influence

Aristotle's Three Components Are as Essential as Rocket Fuel

Just as a rocket ship relies on three foundational elements for its construction and operation, the foundation for persuasion is built upon three core components. Over 2,300 years ago, Aristotle was the first that we know of to identify these components that still underpin effective persuasion today as:

Aristotle's Three Pillars of Persuasion

LOGOS —— Logical Appeal
Your chance to present evidence

ETHOS —— Credibility
Your track record

PATHOS —— Emotional Appeal
Your personal connection

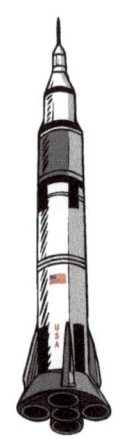

When Decks Become Novels

Do you need proof that businesspeople ignore these principles? After evaluating presentation decks from more than 800 B2B clients, we found something startling: Their decks had as many words as the Bible—but *zero* Emotional Quotient. Our metrics tracked slide count, word count, and "Pathos" (or as we call it, "EQ"). The results were so consistently poor, we eventually stopped counting.

Imagine this: The record for wordiness was set by an unnamed international association with a whopping average of 230 words per slide for an 80-slide deck, totaling over 18,000 words—nearly equal to 65% of this entire book. Now and then, we check incoming content, and sadly, not much has changed. The horrible presentation habits continue through time like a race car stuck in second gear, unable to shift into higher gears, missing every opportunity to accelerate toward success. Understanding and skillfully balancing these core elements can elevate the persuasiveness of any argument, much like the precision engineering that powers a rocket's journey. Yet, some of you will continue to reach for the moon with a rocket fueled by words alone!

The Ethics of Modern Persuasion

Having explored Aristotle's foundational elements of persuasion—Logos, Ethos, and Pathos—let's now shift our focus to the application of these principles in today's world. The power of persuasion, while effective, is often clouded by modern misconceptions, where its misuse in advertising and media has led to widespread mistrust. However, there is a critical distinction between ethical persuasion and manipulation. Understanding this difference is essential as we move toward applying these classical principles in a way that is both powerful and morally sound. To draw this line clearly, we will provide a precise definition of ethical persuasion, building on our earlier definition of storytelling.

> /ˈeTHəkəl / /pərˈswāZH(ə)n/
>
> Ethical persuasion is the process of influencing attitudes, beliefs, or behaviors through communication and messages while demonstrating validity.

Persuasion is a process, and its validity (Ethos) often trips up business presenters. Some rely on unfounded beliefs, while others drown audiences in facts (IQ). Before diving into our *Neuroscience of Persuasion*^{SM} framework and its pillars, let's address the elephant in the room that nearly everyone is aware of, but does little to address. Your overwhelmed, bored audience. They deserve our attention first.

4

Being the Tortoise in Aesop's Fable (Not the Hare)

Proving Stories Didn't Require
a DNA Super Gene

Story: The Currency of Influence

The Early Days

Determining the four cornerstones for the *Neuroscience of Persuasion*[SM] took time. Like Aesop's tortoise, we moved slowly but purposefully. We didn't have a master plan, but we had an audacious goal: to create a solution that would work in the business arena regardless of industry sector or user expertise. The good news for you? We developed hundreds of successful client stories using just Aristotle's components.

Whether you're a dealmaker or an entrepreneur, these basic components of persuasion will serve you well in moving your audience—ethically—from where they are to where you want them to be. One of our early clients, an aviation software company located in the heart of Texas, proved this point. We served them proudly for years, handling every critical communication opportunity (even before we had today's complete framework).

A Texan Teaches in London

Their CEO, Richard, was an industry veteran—a charismatic Texan with a slow southern drawl that could barely keep up with the pace of his brainiac ideas. He called me one day about an upcoming aviation conference in London. Richard knew his Texan dialect and imposing physical presence would draw attention when he took the stage as an event speaker. Our job? Build a persuasive message that embraced who he was.

Because Richard was on stage, we needed to create a warm introduction that built his Ethos (Credibility) quickly without forcing it on his audience and making it relevant to them:

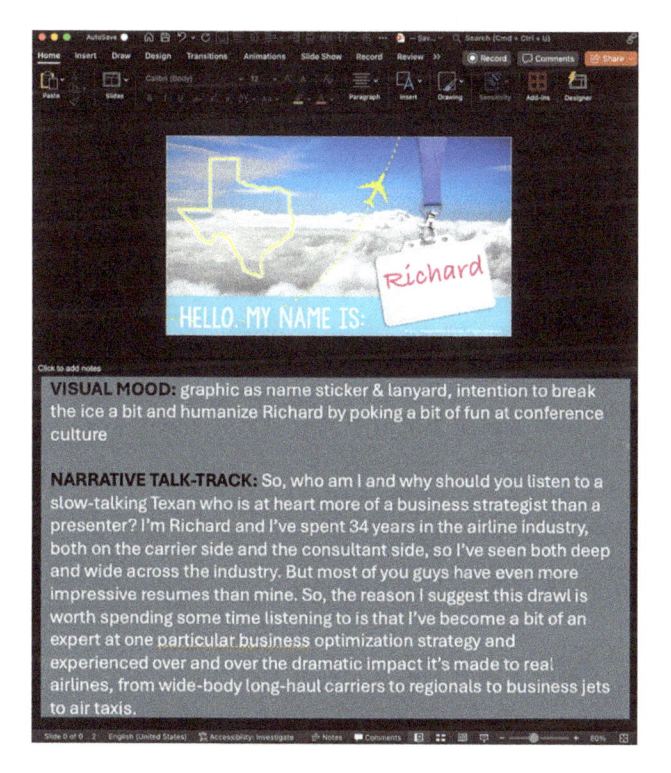

Figure 4.1: Credibility example (Ethos)
from the presenter slides and his narrative talk-track.

The narrative talk-track cleverly builds credibility not by overwhelming with credentials, but by establishing authentic expertise

Story: The Currency of Influence

---

while maintaining approachability—particularly important for a European audience that is potentially skeptical of a Texan speaker. Advancing onward to Aristotle's Pathos, let's establish an emotional connection with his audience.

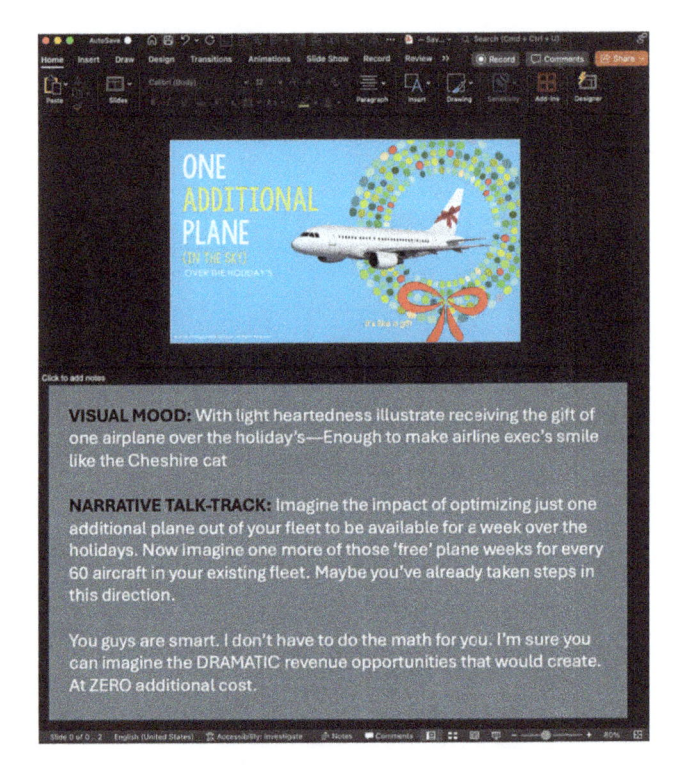

Figure 4.2: Emotional example (Pathos) from the presenter slides and his narrative talk-track.

This emotional journey from Richard moves the audience from delight (holiday gift) to excitement (discovery) to confidence (they're smart enough to see it) to urgency (why aren't we doing this already?)—all while maintaining executive-level sophistication. As we will cover later, increased retention of content exists through a full range of emotions. For you, this means your message is on track to becoming a story because it's memorable. Once you've stirred up the emotions of the audience, it's time to bring in—as my friend Richard would drawl—*them good ol' facts*. Enter Logos.

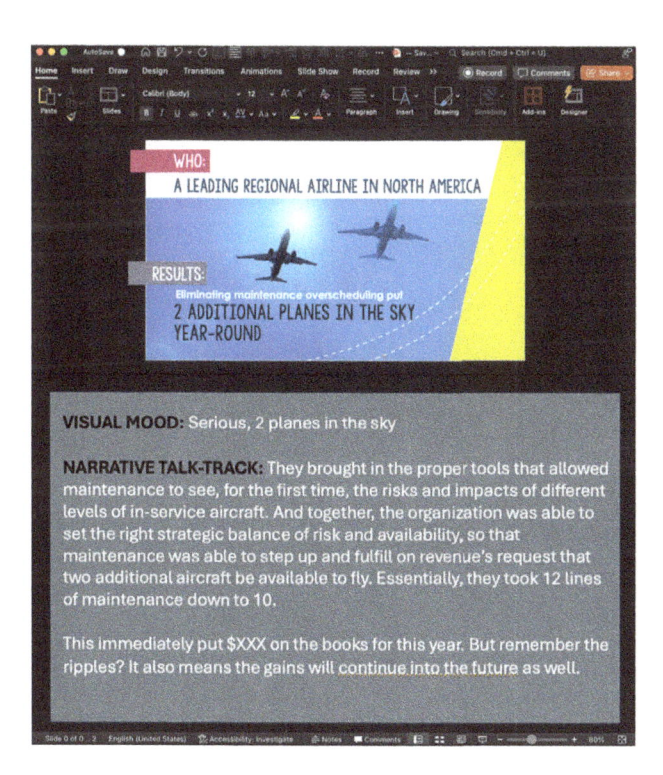

LOGOS

Figure 4.3: Logic example (Logos) from the presenter slides and his narrative talk-track.

Aristotle's components for persuasion help organize undifferentiated content into a persuasive argument for your audience, proving you don't need to be born a storyteller. Like the tortoise, you don't need natural gifts or a DNA super gene—you just need the right approach and the willingness to take steady steps forward. Story is the key. Without a compelling story, even the fastest hare, the most gifted orator, can fail to cross the finish line. Though for us, running an agency focused on storytelling required a more robust framework so that we could efficiently build a variety of stories at the rate of customer need. Think of what you've learned so far as mastering your grip and stance for golf. Now it's time to step onto the practice range and develop your full swing.

5

Your Brain's Factory Settings

Understanding Audience Science

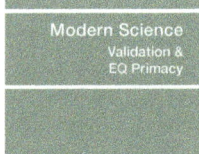

Audience Brain Work

Most of us experience a whirlwind happening in our heads, both through our own internal thoughts and the external bombardments, creating a quagmire of cognitive activity. Given the pervasive nature of content in today's society, audiences now interact more with content than ever before and are harder to impress. Now, let's decode a small scientific adventure—something most people shy away from—to unravel the captivating hypotheses of how emotion influences decision-making in the human brain.

We begin with a term that used to belong strictly to the realm of math nerds and coders: *algorithm*. But today, it's a term that dots the landscape of the boardroom as much as the lab. Many of us businesspeople hold a mindset that our audiences are walking around with secret supercomputers in their heads. It is as if we can and want to absorb overwhelming amounts of content, using algorithmic codes to infinitely process words, metrics, charts, and ideas and make sense of them. **It's a cognitive tsunami before most of us even hit midmorning, swamping us with information overload before our second cup of coffee can kick in.** We may process information well, but humans *are not* algorithms, although the latest advancements in artificial intelligence have us wondering how much longer that statement will be true.

> **It's a cognitive tsunami before most of us even hit midmorning, swamping us with information overload before our second cup of coffee can kick in.**

What They Want Versus What They Get

Imagine a golfer named Jon, and in his spare time, when he's not running a business or writing a book on business storytelling, he sneaks out to the course for a round of golf. After the initial tee shot, in the middle of the fairway (of course), he selects his spade mashie. That's a cool name for the modern-day 6-iron. Jon has an affinity for this club, knows exactly how far he hits it, and has high confidence in executing the golf shot with this club in his hands. However, Jon's overconfidence shows. He knows the yardage and feels sure of the club choice, but he fails to consider other critical factors: the firmness of terrain where the ball should land next, the quality and slope of the lie where the ball lays, nor the wind direction. Just as Jon, the overconfident golfer, misses crucial factors in his golf shots, about 99% of content developers and presenters often overlook how their audience will receive their message. Seems unlikely? Reflect on your last presentation: What percentage of the total development did you dedicate to the consideration of your audience? **When less than half of your prep time focuses on your audience, you're not telling their story—you're just selling your capabilities.** And this, my friends, translates into an undifferentiated view for your audience because your focus is on yourself, when it needs to be on them.

> When less than half of your prep time focuses on your audience, you're not telling their story—you're just selling your capabilities.

No one knows how often opportunity knocks, but when we hear that knock, there should be a concerted effort to open the door. In a business context, professional audiences are often forced to listen to our mundane presentations, but desperately hope for something better. That has been the focus of our agency since the early 2000s. We have touted some empirical data to support this; however, statistics are often skewed toward a biased preference. So rather than offer you a statistic to prove this point, let's get introspective and personal. Consider posing this question to any business group the next time you are sharing a room: *How many of you would prefer today's message presented to you in a narrative-based story versus the usual business dump?* Although there are exceptions, the result is clear: rarely, if ever, will less than 50% of the room prefer a narrative-based story.

Now, switch to your *audience* hat for a minute. In the last 10 presentations that you have watched, how many have delivered the presentation with a narrative-driven story? Do you remember them? How many important points stand out? Were there many presenters you felt connected with enough to trust? No doubt, very few have done this, and you see where this is going. The audience wants the story far more than we provide it. For those businesspeople seeking differentiation, this gap between what the audiences desire—story—versus what they get, too much biz gibberish, should resonate with us. For those who fail to see the significance of this opportunity gap—well, let's just hope they're your competition. With lost deal opportunities, people place the fault on the product or service solution, and sometimes that is true, but in those commoditized situations, we cannot ignore the inability to construct the best dynamic narratives and tell stories that excite the brain of your audience. The primary driver behind the audience's millennia-old desire to crave a story is the wonderful, magnificent brain.

Unveiling the Biological Brain

The most attention-grabbing aspect of our biological brains is the astonishing statistic that a simple piece of brain tissue, the size of a grain of sand, contains 100,000 neurons and 1 billion synapses. However, the most relevant efforts today are from scientists like Alan Jasanoff, who are bringing attention to the idea that the brain is not a supercomputer, but a biological and instinctual organ composed mostly of fat. In his book *The Biological Mind*, Jasanoff challenges the common notion of the brain as a separate, dominant entity controlling the body. He argues that this perspective is scientifically inaccurate, emphasizing that the brain's functions are deeply intertwined with the body and environment. Jasanoff explains, "If part of what makes you include your emotional side, your physical abilities, and the decisions you make, then it is scientifically inaccurate to equate yourself to your brain." This statement highlights the integrated nature of the mind, body, and environment, urging a move away from viewing the brain in isolation. **Your brain isn't the boss; it's part of the team.** This perspective is particularly relevant to business executives, reminding them to consider the holistic nature of human behavior in their decision-making and interactions.

This process is intricate, involving multiple parts of the brain and drawing influence from neurotransmitters, hormones, and genetics, alongside environmental factors. In the next section, we'll dive into how neurotransmitters affect communication, but for now, we'll focus on how the brain naturally responds to positivity versus negativity in messaging. Understanding this reaction is essential for effectively engaging your audience.

> **Your brain isn't the boss; it's part of the team.**

What Your Audience Feels Is More Relevant than What You Believe They Think

As we mature, our brains develop a record of negative response patterns that warn us to stay out of harm's way—don't touch that hot pan! Life's repeated patterns train us to trust our brains as advisors when something might be amiss in our environment. When our communication intake is solely positivity, this can trigger a sense of disbelief, like reading only 5-star reviews. That 3-pound lump of biology inside our heads is triangulating any external signals plus our past patterned negative experiences. Yes, danger or significant downside might be lurking. After all, your author is typing this chapter on a cross-country flight, wondering if someone evil has indeed released venomous *Snakes on a Plane*. What your business audience *feels* is more relevant than what you believe they think.

Business leaders often stumble when they forget a basic truth about human nature: people decide with both their heads and their hearts. Nowhere is this clearer than in publicly traded companies, where leadership sometimes tries to control the narrative by banning all negative statements. Their logic seems sound—after all, institutional analysts can trigger stock sell-offs with a single negative report. But this mandate for positivity-only messaging becomes toxic in high-stakes deals. When potential clients hearing your pitch catch nothing but sunshine and flowers in a multimillion-dollar negotiation, they don't just doubt your story—they doubt your credibility. They know business has risks. By pretending it doesn't, you've lost them.

In another part of the same company, a different executive might embrace this same edict to eliminate negativity in communications. The problem? Their audience is skeptical decision-makers, who doubt any implementation will be problem free. When mature audiences encounter only positives, their biological response triggers skepticism—either fearing catastrophe or disbelieving the promised utopia. Our brains make these doubts impossible to ignore.

When we only show the good, we leave our skeptical client audience to imagine the bad. Building trust requires acknowledging downsides. Including brief notes about potential risks helps your audience connect with your humanity and shows them the complete story, not just a glossed-over version.

> **When we only show the good, we leave our skeptical client audience to imagine the bad.**

One cannot place too much emphasis exclusively upon one extreme emotion without considering the external environment, in this case, the potential mindset of your audience. An approach that resonates with our brains is a balanced, authentic presentation of both positive and negative aspects. For instance, this year's new race car design might offer increased race pace and competitive advantage, but there's a caveat—the brakes may overheat during slow corners. Acknowledging this, the race engineer advises the race car driver to periodically coast and downshift to maintain brake temperature. This honesty not only initiates the trust-building process but also enhances the chances of winning by preparing the driver for potential risks, such as brake failure leading to a crash. Imagine if the race engineer didn't share this info because his job was on the line. Getting the race car driver to faster lap times was a performance metric that solidified the engineer's job security. In the seller-buyer business world, this type of "in-it-for-me" mentality is commonplace.

Businesspeople who want to win at storytelling would do well to recognize the instinctual balance humans crave. Just as a skilled race car driver navigates both the thrills and dangers of the track, effective communicators must navigate the complexities of human emotion guided by our biological brains. Crafting a narrative that embraces both positivity and challenges fosters deeper connections with audiences and lays the foundation for trust. **Trust deepens when your narrative honestly weaves together both victories and challenges.** Yet, if you enjoy high-stakes risk, then paint that all-too-rosy picture in your next pitch and let the dice roll.

Safety First

Crashing a race car benefits only parts suppliers. Similarly, humans instinctively avoid crashes—both vehicular and metaphorical. Abraham Maslow's groundbreaking 1954 book on human motivation, *Motivation and Personality*, shows that once we satisfy our basic survival needs,

> **Trust deepens when your narrative honestly weaves together both victories and challenges.**

maintaining that safety becomes our primary concern. We cling to this safety so tightly that reaching for something more brings apprehension. Put most of us in a Formula 1 car, and we'd drive nice and slow, avoiding any risk of a crash. This same instinct affects business decisions.

This safety-first approach directly influences our decision-making processes. Our brains are constantly engaged in the important task of filtering out irrelevant information, to preserve our limited cognitive capacity.[7] With approximately 70,000 thoughts per day, the brain sifts through a flood of sensory inputs, especially when faced with complex scenarios, like a business proposal. In these moments, people instinctively gravitate toward cognitive shortcuts, favoring safety over complex solutions. Just as a race car driver avoids unnecessary risks, your business decision-makers prioritize risk mitigation over innovation. Consider you're in the coffee bean sourcing industry: Before you tell them how great your Peruvian coffee beans are, consider their fear of a far-flung supply chain not meeting deliveries and the impact to their business unit quarterly performance numbers.

Understanding the psychological motivations behind safety and using storytelling to align with your audience's mindset are essential steps in presenting a message that resonates deeply. **Humans default to cognitive shortcuts when navigating both complexity and safety concerns.** Translation for the business presenter: Your proposal needs to be easy to understand and consider the audience's position of safety.

> **Humans default to cognitive shortcuts when navigating both complexity and safety concerns.**

Understanding your audience's preexisting mindset and weaving these realities into your message creates valuable alignment. When

---

[7] Plebanek, D. J., and V. M. Sloutsky, "Selective Attention, Filtering, and the Development of Working Memory," *Developmental Science* 22, no. 1 (2019): DOI: 10.1111/desc.12727.

paired with storytelling, this becomes today's currency of influence—making complex ideas digestible and winning over your audience.

Merging Mind and Matter

Understanding storytelling starts with recognizing that your audience can't process information like a supercomputer. They crave stories, yet businesses keep force-feeding them empty calories of data. The competitive knockout blow lies in simplification—recognizing their limited resources to decipher complexities. Einstein's wisdom applies perfectly here: "Make everything as simple as possible, but not simpler." But clarity alone isn't enough to tell the best story. As we'll explore in the next chapter, your audience's *feelings* are just as crucial to winning deals.

6

Your Audience Is Not a Hard Drive

Cognitive Load

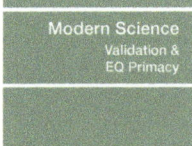

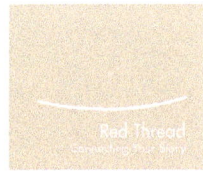

Miss Their Brain's Signals of Survive and Thrive, and Miss Your Deal

As the highest life-forms on Earth, it's crucial for us as speakers to tap into the workings of the human brain. Our intellectual abilities and desire for practical reasoning distinguish us from other creatures and are vital for our brain's primary missions: survival and thriving. Recognizing how, as humans, we function in situations such as pitching a business proposal or raising capital can enhance our endeavors. It's like having a piece of the other team's game plan. It should be impossible to ignore.

For example, with food choices, we rely on practical reasoning. My dog and I share an unwavering enthusiasm for bacon, and we both understand the importance of food for survival. Unlike my beloved hundred-pound furry eating machine, who indulges without restraint, I can use practical reasoning to aim for a healthier lifestyle and avoid overindulging in bacon before I oink. But when I'm truly hungry, my higher reasoning can fail, and suddenly I'm competing slice-for-slice with my canine friend. This same survival-versus-thriving tension affects your audience during oral presentations. When they're under pressure from looming deadlines, skipped lunches causing ravenous bellies, or meetings that keep them from catching flights, their higher-order thinking suffers. Just as my reasoning about bacon falters when I'm starving, your audience's ability to focus on thriving goals diminishes when basic needs aren't met. Our brain's primary inclination is survival-based, with thriving only becoming meaningful after ensuring survival. In a business context, consider Will Rogers's wisdom: "It's not the return on my investment that I am concerned about; it's the return of my investment." He wants to preserve his original money. In other words, as dealmakers we'd do well to lock in on our audience's basic survival needs first and thriving aspirations second.

Nearly all human actions follow the brain's twin missions: to survive and to thrive. The rewards of thriving—accolades and comfort—are a powerful draw. Yet, our primal survival instinct takes precedence, often overpowering the desire to thrive by instinctively resisting changes that could threaten our safety. As presenters, it's crucial to recognize that our proposals, at least in part, might come across to the audience as threats to their sense of security, even if the initial request for proposal was the client's aspiration. For now, let's temporarily park this thought of survival and safety. Unlike my bacon-obsessed dog who operates purely on instinct, we humans can harness both reason and emotion—not just to moderate our bacon cravings, but also for unraveling how emotions and brain mechanics prime us for effective storytelling.

Dopamine and the Invisible Influence

Humans possess a biological reward system that has taught us to repeat activities that bring about pleasure. These are things that enable us to survive or thrive, as well as discourage us with extra bad feelings when we do something that might get us eaten by a tiger.[8]

The reward that we are chasing is the neurotransmitter dopamine. Long before man learned to cultivate or manufacture pharmaceuticals, rye whiskey, or substances to light on fire and smoke, dopamine was the original wonder drug, and it was free. When it's triggered, we feel strong positive emotions—happiness, hope, motivation, awe—that let

---

[8] Wang, F., J. Yang, F. Pan, R. C. Ho, and J. H. Huang, "Editorial: Neurotransmitters and Emotions," *Frontiers in Psychology* 11 (January 28, 2020). DOI: 10.3389/fpsyg.2020.00021.

us know we're making the right decisions and encourage us to act.[9] For the presenter, effectively tapping into your audience's emotions is the holy grail of memorable storytelling. Achieving this requires a shift in the presenter's approach: moving away from simply aiming to shape the audience's thoughts about the outcomes, to harnessing emotive *feelings* that resonate with their situation. The key to mastering memorable storytelling is to realize that it's not about promoting your solution but connecting with their situation, and your narrative and content must reflect this understanding.

Why emphasize evoking emotions in an audience? Emotionally charged presentations capture attention, which is crucial with limited cognitive resources. Initially, presenters who inspire us emotionally have our full and rapt attention.[10] [11] Considering our overtaxed cognitive resources, gaining the audience's attention is job number one. Secondarily, if you have delivered something emotively charged to the audience, you've increased their chance of remembering it. But that's not all; John Medina, author of *Brain Rules* and the founder of two brain research institutes, states, "Emotions anchor memories—making them last longer and stay clearer than neutral events." This is where most businesspeople choose comfort, staying solely with what they know and likely staying behind their competition. If you want your audience to have an accurate mental sticky note about your technology pitch deck, then building an emotionally charged narrative is your race car's slipstream to pass the competition and cross the finish line first.

I remember exactly where I was when Formula 1's reigning king, Ayrton Senna, died. On that warm spring Sunday in 1994, I sat on

---

[9] Wang et al., "Editorial: Neurotransmitters and Emotions," DOI: 10.3389/fpsyg.2020.00021.

[10] Ferrari V., N. Bruno, R. Chattat, and M. Codispoti, "Evaluative Ratings and Attention across the Life Span: Emotional Arousal and Gender," *Cognition and Emotion* 31, no. 3 (2017): 552–563. DOI: 10.1080/02699931.2016.1140020.

[11] Miller C. J., J. McNear, and M. J. Metz, "A Comparison of Traditional and Engaging Lecture Methods in a Large, Professional-Level Course," *Advances in Physiology Education* 37, no. 4 (2013): 347–355. DOI: 10.1152/advan.00050.2013.

my way-too-shiny blue couch, staring at a sporting news broadcast in disbelief. The three-time world champion and most electrifying driver of his generation had just crashed at Imola's turn 3. My month-old son slept nearby in his wooden crib, unknowingly named after another Brazilian racing legend, Emerson Fittipaldi. The irony wasn't lost on me—one Brazilian champion's namesake peacefully dreaming while another champion's life ended on a racetrack half a world away. I'd planned on playing golf that afternoon but found myself frozen in front of our 400-pound TV on its swivel stand, right next to the brick fireplace still in need of cleaning, as motorsport lost one of its greatest icons.

Nearly three decades later, it has etched a detailed, lasting visual and emotional memory, highlighting how powerfully such events embed themselves in our consciousness. Chances are that your next pitch will not evoke the gut-wrenching emotions of life and death, but it's also unlikely that your presentation needs to be remembered by your audience three decades later. Success might be as simple as having your pitch vividly remembered by the C-suite three weeks after you delivered it. How can you harness this type of emotive energy in your presentation? Try conjuring some dopamine from thin air. It is an invisible powerhouse, and it's there in the minds of your audience, just waiting for the presenter who wants to tell the best stories to activate it.

Ignore Mirror Neurons, Lose Your Connection

Mirror neurons are a type of brain cell that reacts both when an individual performs an action and when they observe someone else who performs the same action. This mirroring mechanism enables us to empathize and understand the emotions and intentions of others, creating a sort of "chameleon-like" experience of others' feelings. Mirror neurons are intricately linked to emotion because feelings are how we interpret our emotions. For example, when watching your favorite professional golfer on television demonstrate an energetic fist pump after scoring a hole in one, you may feel an energetic twinge yourself, even though you are not in the same situation. But before we delve into these neurons and their relevance for presenters, let's establish our understanding of emotion itself.

Asking scientists to agree on the definition of emotion is like asking teenagers to surrender their phones at the dinner table—you're in for a struggle. Classical theories insist emotions are universal and innate, lying in wait like that single branch in an otherwise empty sky that somehow manages to knock down my perfect golf shot. But neuroscientist Lisa Feldman Barrett challenges this view in her *Theory of Constructed Emotion*. Her revolutionary research suggests something that might upset both scientists and golfers throwing clubs after hitting trees. While emotions feel automatic and universal, the scientific evidence tells a different story.

Lisa Barrett's theory highlights an intricate dance between the brain, body, and cultural environment in constructing your emotions. This interaction results in a unique emotional landscape for each individual, largely driven by the brain's predictions and the continuous feedback loop that either confirms or adjusts these predictions. Mirror neurons play a crucial role in this process, working alongside the brain's predictive behavior. Our brain uses experiences and observations to anticipate and understand the actions and emotions of others, facilitating social interactions and empathetic responses.

I was once painfully blindsided on the football field by a vicious tackle. My brain, in part with my body and environment and likely millions of other sensory loops, constructed this as what sudden and shocking pain from collision feels like. So, when I'm driving—probably too fast—down the highway and I witness a car crash well ahead of me, my visceral reaction is to wince in pain. Pain that my brain associated with my experiences, like the football field, can resurface. I wasn't in the car collision, but I momentarily felt what I believed the other people in the car crash were feeling. These are mirror neurons in play.

Your Audience Will Match Your Energy, for Better or Worse

When your company invites an expert speaker, you might find yourself feeling particularly energized, uplifted, and motivated to tackle the rest of the day with vigor and determination after their presentation. This isn't your first experience with such talks, but this time, something's different. Often, it's not the content of the speech that invigorates you, but how the speaker's emotions make you feel. This is because when a speaker displays uplifting and positive emotions, their audience mimics these emotions because of mirror neurons.

Your Vibe Attracts Your Tribe

I've got this friend, an investor and C-suite whisperer, and we occasionally grab lunch together. He's the guy with a Rolodex that reads like a Who's Who of celebrities and business moguls—always looking at the world as a playground of endless opportunities. Global pandemic knocking at the door? He's busy plotting a strategic pivot. Supply chains in disarray? He's sketching out ways in his trusty composition notebook to streamline and boost throughput. His brainstorms often find their way into his loyal scribble sidekick, sometimes clear as day, other times more like a cryptic puzzle that I cannot interpret even after a full bottle of Côtes du Rhône. But here's the kicker: Every time we part ways, I head in the other direction, infused with a *feeling*. Somehow, his emotional attitude of unconstrained opportunities is contagious. However, if I said to my friend, "I'm in a low place right now; please motivate me," he'd flounder like a fish on a hot sidewalk. That's the magic of mirror neurons—you catch the vibe you hang around with, so stay away from stranded fish, find yourself an energized friend, and know you attract ... or repel with your behavior.

Plant Emotion, Harvest Results

As a storyteller, your task extends beyond merely strategically pressing the emotional buttons of your audience; it involves authentically conveying your own. Presenting a dry, fact-only message, even if you believe your offerings outshine the competition, will likely elicit a similarly unenthusiastic dry response from your audience. This approach for a deal opportunity reduces your pitch to a mere transaction, whereas establishing a trusting relationship—built through emotion—is key to securing the deal.

Let's make this clear: The probability of mirror neurons exists within your audience. They can either work for you or against you. Plant a broad spectrum of emotions at the feet of your audience. This will encourage your audience to easily recall your message more accurately. This nuanced emotional engagement sets exceptional storytellers apart and captivates their audiences.

Avoiding the Emotional Stall

In synthesizing brainwork in this section, we should guard against oversimplifying our approach for the sake of storytelling. Science takes us well beyond creating emotional or enthusiastic narratives. Like the best novels and movies, effective business stories should encompass a range of emotions and never lose sight of your audience's brain's dual mission to survive and thrive. Your business stories should do the same. As a guideline, consider this spectrum of emotions along with the following story about how to effectively intermingle realistic emotional stages in a narrative:

Four Emotions That Make Stories Stick

Presenter Emotion: CONCERN AND TENSION
"Plant the Stakes"
1. Start by highlighting concern and tension, focusing on survival challenges in an ever-changing market.

Presenter Emotion: JOY OF ILLUMINATION
"Paint Their Perfect World"
2. Avoiding the specificity of your company's solution, introduce the emotion of joy by painting thriving outcomes in their market. Create this vision as if the audience had a magic wand to solve their problems.

Presenter Emotion: VULNERABILITY
"Share Your Scars"
3. Acknowledge our human inclinations to imagine bad outcomes when only presented with the good. We preempt this emotional feeling by incorporating vulnerability.

Presenter Emotion: BALANCED OPTIMISM
"Balance Their Hope"
4. Conclude by returning to the primal concern, the theme of survival. Keep a balanced sense of optimism. Ensure emotional stability without sacrificing the pursuit of thriving.

Story: The Currency of Influence

A recent experience at an Atlanta restaurant located by the melodically named Chattahoochee River perfectly illustrates this emotional spectrum. After lunch, as my business friend and I parted in the parking lot, I mentioned his upcoming event, casually warning him with a few specifics not to let it mirror a near-fatal hunting incident he'd experienced eight months ago on another continent. "Newsome. Oh my gosh, your memory is incredible!" he exclaimed. As I got into my car I basked in the praise until a wrong-way driver forced me to dodge, my imaginary F1 racing reflexes kicking in. Miles down the road, humility struck. It wasn't my memory that was remarkable—it was his storytelling that made that eight-month-old event unforgettable. Like the *Snakes on a Plane* movie, my brain had stored his vivid tale in the hippocampus as a survival lesson, precisely because his story had masterfully touched all four emotional ranges that we discussed earlier:

Breaking Down the Complexity of Rocket Science

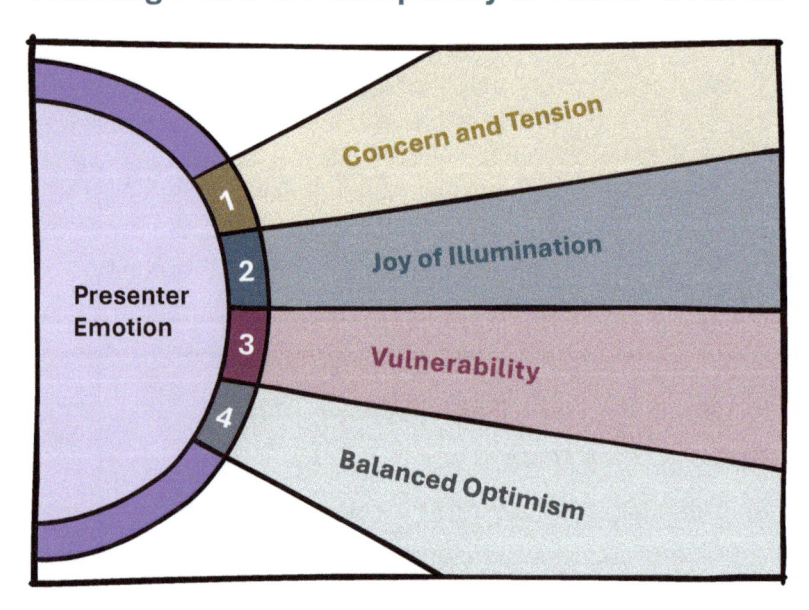

Figure 6.1: As you watch your next show, make a mental note and you'll likely see a wide range of emotions, like the illustration above.

48

For my friend's story those emotions began with *concern and tension*—a near-death experience from a hemothorax while visiting another continent. Despite the danger, he survived, offering a sense of *joy of illumination*. In reflecting on the event, he acknowledged a newfound *vulnerability*, realizing that his physical coordination, while still impressive for his age, was no longer as sharp as it had been in his youth. Finally, he expressed a desire to return to the same place, driven by *balanced optimism* for a chance at measured redemption. By attentively considering these emotional ranges, you will probably have trumped your competition, creating a story that's more than just rah-rah emotions. It will be a rich, engaging narrative that leaves your audience *feeling* something with a short, compelling, and memorable winning story.

7

Emotion Is the Potion

Your Audience Is Why You're There

Story: The Currency of Influence

Give Them a Personal Stake, or Let Them Sleep

If I start a presentation by saying, "My brand of coffee is made from ethically farmed rich beans," or "My brand of coffee is chosen by restaurants everywhere," I've just given you an option or maybe a fact that you may not care about. If I say instead, "I suspect that within your morning routine as you get your day started, I know how satisfying it is to start your day off right with a great cup of coffee, and the last thing you want is to begin with something less than you deserve," I've started a narrative that gives you a *personal stake* in the information that follows. Advertisers have been so successful in employing this strategy that we spend more than $120 billion with them every year to make our companies more successful. However, their techniques are available to anyone who can imagine what an audience needs.

Figure 7.1: The left thought bubble represents a presenter focused on product features or solutions, while the right illustrates the effective strategy of aligning with the audience about their preferences, ensuring relevance and engagement.

Whenever we mention the coffee example during training, there's invariably a well-meaning businessperson who points out, with a touch of cynicism, that their field is far more complex than selling coffee. I must take a moment to apologize to a friend in the coffee industry for possibly underselling their craft. These coffee maestros have transformed a humble cup of joe into a global obsession, coaxing consumers to fork over $32 a week for something like an iced brown sugar oat milk shaken espresso. While some might dismiss the coffee example as too simplistic for their complex business offerings, the principle remains the same—it's about the audience's perspective, not your content. This is where most people stumble when they sit down to create their presentations.

The content developers' mistake is that they focus on the information they want to convey. We alluded earlier to this haphazard approach with what Professor McEnerney from the University of Chicago emphasizes to his graduate students: the fallacy of believing that good writing is simply about presenting one's own ideas clearly. It's not just students, businesspeople, or government employees who fall into this trap; it's a common tendency in human nature. Most businesspeople have advanced their business career without being formally taught how to tailor content to the audience's perspective. Unfortunately, as humans, we often write or create content based on what we want to express without adequately considering the viewpoint of those who are reading or listening. As we move forward, let's explore how we can shift our focus from a presenter-centered approach to constructing content that truly resonates with our audience.

Story: The Currency of Influence

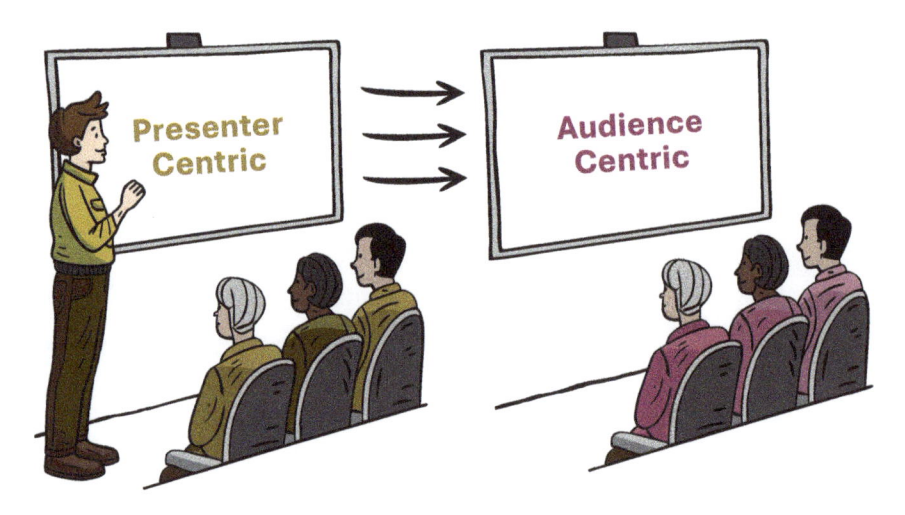

Figure 7.2: Shifting presentation content to focus on the audience.

We have all sat in that conference room or auditorium, watching a boring presenter drone on, thinking that poking ourselves in the eye might be preferable to enduring a barrage of bullet points that have no personal relevance. How did the presenter end up here, you might ask? Likely a Frankenstein process combination of copy and paste, slide transfers from other decks, and building the rest of the content spontaneously slide after slide.

When successful presenters begin a presentation, they chart out what their audience feels at the start before they put the first word on a slide. These champion presenters put any existing content aside and shift to understanding the audience. This is significantly more than understanding audience demographics. It is who they are as humans and what emotions they might deal with. It's like a racing team preparing their vehicle before a race, focusing not just on the aerodynamics or mechanics but also on the track conditions, the weather, and the competition's potential strategies. Similarly, these presenters distill their message, ensuring it's calibrated to resonate with their wide-ranging emotions, with a goal of knowing where the finish line is for the audience and not just themselves.

Contrary to popular belief, great presenters are not silver-tongued word processors. They devote more time to audience discovery because it's how they know they can get a leg up on their competition. Understanding that audiences are often the most overlooked yet critical element of presenting, these presenters possess a keen sense of awareness that their audience is never in a state of mind to absorb 100% of anybody's content. As members of the audience, what's keeping us from zeroing in on the presenter?

Humans can only process a fraction of the 11 million pieces of input we receive every moment. This number might seem arbitrary, as it depends on how one defines "fragments." Consider this: back in 2009, when companies were still selling floppy disks (ask your parents if you're unfamiliar), the University of California San Diego reported that the average American consumed 100,000 words per day or about 34 gigabytes of information. But we know this number has increased significantly since then.

In 2009, an estimated 100,000 developer apps were available for download through our shiny new smartphone devices. Today, that number has skyrocketed to over 5.1 million. More apps translate to increased time spent online, where the onslaught of information "fragments" begin their bombardment run on our minds. On average, our eyeballs connect to the internet for 4.11 hours per day[12], a number that has been growing at a 6.5% CAGR since 2009. Based on this rough calculation, in 2025, we'd be consuming over 257,000 words daily and 85 gigabytes of information, nearly 2.5 times more than in 2009.

You should be feeling overwhelmed, thinking about how much content is haplessly thrown at you daily. That's exactly how an audience feels when a well-meaning business presenter crams 150+ words onto each of their 30 boring slides. The presenter is thinking solely about

---

[12] Wermsur, Yoram, "The Majority of Americans' Mobile Time Spent Takes Place in Apps," eMarketer.com, July 2020, https://www.emarketer.com/content/the-majority-of-americans-mobile-time-spent-takes-place-in-apps.

their "goodies," and, unlike the aware master dealmaker, the average presenter is not giving much thought to what their audience is dealing with. With audiences drowning in this tsunami of daily information, understanding how their brains filter content isn't just helpful—it's critical to your success.

Their Brains Are Filtering You Out

Figure 7.3: What our brains are dealing with every waking minute of our days.

We're bombarded with sensory information every minute of every day, far more than we can reliably process at once. It's crucial to understand how our brains manage this influx. Research by Professors Plebanek and Sloutsky sheds light on the process, revealing that our ability to filter out irrelevant information, known as filtering efficiency, is a key factor in our working memory capacity.[13] This capacity, however,

---

[13] Plebanek, Daniel J., and Vladimir M. Sloutsky, "Selective Attention, Filtering, and the Development of Working Memory," *Developmental Science* 22(1) (2019): e12727. DOI: 10.1111/desc.12727.

reaches its peak around age 7. As a result, our brains are constantly engaged today in sifting through the deluge of the daily 11 million fragments, relying on filtering efficiency to discard the nonessential.

This has significant implications for business presenters. Your audience members have varying abilities to filter and process information—some may absorb complex material quickly, while others might struggle with the same content. To communicate effectively, presenters must adapt their message to be accessible to everyone, including those with the least capacity to filter complex information. This means simplifying multifaceted points, emphasizing key takeaways, and engaging all sensory channels to maximize retention.

Our brains constantly search for relevance, asking, "What does this mean for me?" When presentations lack personal significance, attention wanders. Research shows that maintaining audience engagement isn't about arbitrary time limits or attention-span myths. **For the presenter, grabbing and holding the audience's attention requires relevancy, interactive elements, and thoughtful preparation.**[14] [15] And here's what many presenters miss: The most compelling presentations aren't necessarily the shortest—they're the ones that matter most to their audience.

> **For the presenter, grabbing and holding the audience's attention requires relevancy, interactive elements, and thoughtful preparation.**

In today's world, which is overflowing with information, it's crucial to grasp how our brains filter content. When delivering presentations

---

[14] Miller, C. J., J. McNear, and M. J. Metz, "A Comparison of Traditional and Engaging Lecture Methods in a Large, Professional-Level Course," *Advances in Physiology Education* 37, no. 4 (2013): 347–355. DOI: 10.1152/advan.00050.2013.

[15] Bradbury, N. A., "Attention Span During Lectures: 8 Seconds, 10 Minutes, or More?" *Advances in Physiology Education* 40, no. 4 (2016): 509–513. DOI: 10.1152/advan.00109.2016.

in business settings, it's important for speakers to customize their messages to capture the interest of all listeners, regardless of their varying attention capacities, by creating relevance and encouraging interaction. One way to accomplish this is understanding the emotions of our audience and through the application of emotive language, both the spoken word and the typography of a presentation document. Let us go on an adventure for emotive content, shall we?

8

The Audience Whisperer

Uncomplicating Your Audience

Story: The Currency of Influence

The Audience Emotion Navigator

Imagine an enterprise on the hunt for a financial planning and analysis platform, sending out a request for proposals (RFP) to a half dozen hopeful providers. They're asking for strategy, deployment, project management, economic considerations, and a laundry list of other requirements. The submission will be a hefty stack of documents, but lurking in the shadows is a presentation file. This file has the potential to either resemble Tolstoy's *War and Peace*, turning the potential client's mind into a bowl of alphabet soup, or a pitch deck that delivers a memorable, distilled story arc that stands out from the competition and is easily digestible by the review team. We shall focus on this later for the sake of our often-beleaguered audience.

Remember, even a complex rocket ship has foundational core elements, and so does audience discovery. To create a personal connection with the audience, we divide their needs into three categories: their focus, hopes, and fears. But modern business decisions rarely rest with a single decision-maker. Instead, they involve multiple layers of influence—from industry-wide concerns to leadership priorities to individual stakeholder needs. By cross-referencing these three audience levels with our three need categories, we create a 9-grid matrix we affectionately call the *Emotion Map*, as shown in Figure 8.1. Beyond the obvious table stakes, this map finally offers business development teams a way to shift focus from endlessly polishing their own shiny products to something truly revolutionary: paying attention to the emotional states of the client. It's a fun (and overdue) exercise that forces teams to stop making assumptions and instead determine what emotional positions the person across the table holds, which, spoiler alert, might just matter more than how slick your pitch deck looks. Now that we understand how audiences filter information, we need a navigation system to help us get through those filters. Think of it as a GPS for your audience's emotional terrain.

The Emotion Map

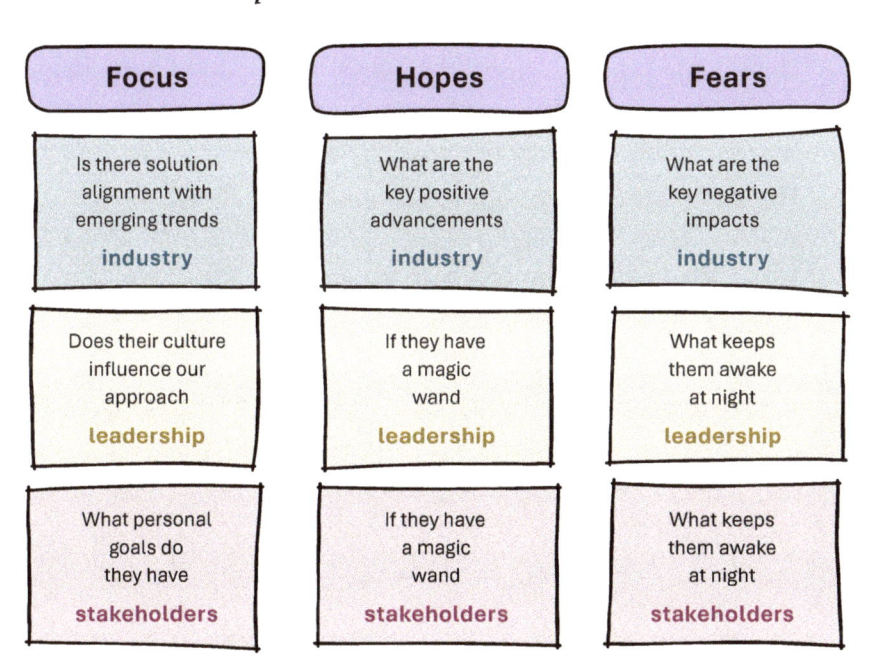

Focus	Hopes	Fears
Is there solution alignment with emerging trends **industry**	What are the key positive advancements **industry**	What are the key negative impacts **industry**
Does their culture influence our approach **leadership**	If they have a magic wand **leadership**	What keeps them awake at night **leadership**
What personal goals do they have **stakeholders**	If they have a magic wand **stakeholders**	What keeps them awake at night **stakeholders**

Figure 8.1: The *Emotion Map* aligns key feelings across industry and levels within an organization.

The *Emotion Map* might look complex at first glance, but like any excellent strategy, it comes to life in three key elements. Working through this mechanism (using a fictitious example), the information in our scenario applied to the following framework of the *Emotion Map* would look something like this:

Three Steps to Core Emotion

Now, let's consider how to use the *Emotion Map* effectively, without getting bogged down in unnecessary details. The map is broken down into three emotional categories—**focus, hopes, and fears**—each viewed through three audience lenses: the **industry**, the **leadership**, and the **stakeholders**.

Here's how this can be applied:

1. **Focus:** What is top of mind for each group? In an industry struggling with regulatory changes, focus might be on how to remain compliant. Leadership, on the other hand, might zero in on improving communication between departments, while stakeholders could concentrate on gaining more personal expertise.

2. **Hopes:** What do they hope to achieve? The industry might look to innovate and adopt new trends, while leadership might hope for long-term financial growth. Stakeholders may aspire to be seen as thought leaders in their field, with a desire to drive collaboration and improve planning.

3. **Fears:** What are their worst-case scenarios? The industry fears being labeled as a legacy sector that's fallen behind more innovative industries. Leadership fears resistance to change within the organization, and stakeholders fear the consequences of poor decision-making or being overwhelmed by complex financial data.

By framing your narrative around these emotional drivers, you speak directly to their core concerns, aligning your pitch with their underlying needs.

We have carried out this initial audience evaluation with clients on countless occasions, engaging in 30 to 45 minutes of collaborative brainstorming with a select group of individuals connected to the client. While we teach advanced techniques in some workshops—just running through this questioning exercise stretches the muscle needed to better form an EQ snapshot of your audience.

This is very much a discovery phase to gain the critical emotional quotient (EQ) bridge to connect personally with them. However, sometimes, there is no prior customer relationship, which implies that our clients must undertake research, such as canvassing the internet to identify the key contacts, understand the company's positioning, and become informed about recent industry developments and trends. Captivating storytellers demand to understand the audience in the fullest possible way, thinking about every path in their orbit.

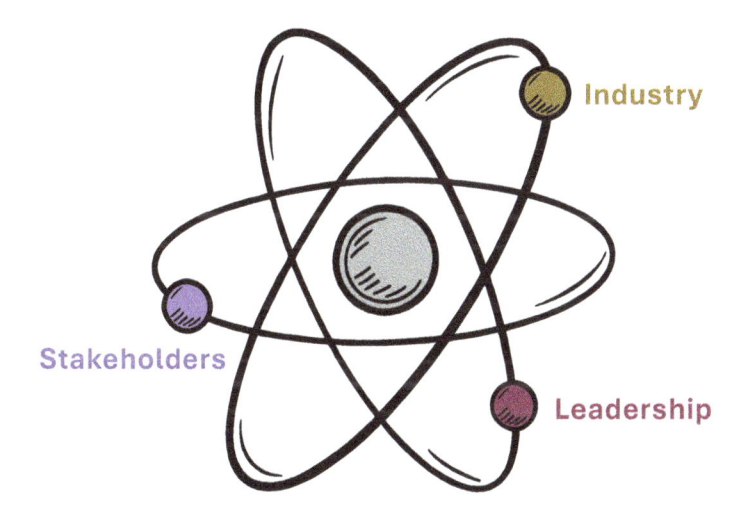

Figure 8.2: The *Emotion Map* effectively considers multiple paths that exist in the orbit of your audience, considering emotions spanning from the broadest perspective (industry) to the narrowest (stakeholder).

Remember, your audience has a human brain trying to focus by asking the question, "What does this mean for me?"

The Gears of Connection

Understanding that you can divide your audience into three emotional levels is crucial, but here's where most presenters make a critical

Story: The Currency of Influence

> **Rushing through the biological gears of communication is like forcing a car into high gear too soon—both actions disrupt the natural flow between presenter and audience.**

mistake—they try to shift into high gear too quickly, away from the emotional side of their audience, treating it like a checkbox. Anybody who has driven a manual transmission vehicle knows the feeling of prematurely shifting into a higher gear. This is where you're expecting to continue the acceleration path, but the engine simply isn't ready to support it. **Rushing through the biological gears of communication is like forcing a car into high gear too soon—both actions disrupt the natural flow between presenter and audience.** The vast majority, your competition, but not likely you, arrive to second gear prematurely, a mistake that diminishes the humanity of their audience, mistakenly pretending they are an algorithm and are only interested in the numbers.

Gears of Persuasion
Sequential Transitions

1 3
R 2 4

Concern and Tension
Joy of Illumination
Vulnerability
Balanced Optimism

Failing to progress through the biological gears of communication mirrors the struggle of a car stalling when prematurely shifting into a higher gear, a misstep that disrupts the dynamic between presenters and their audience.

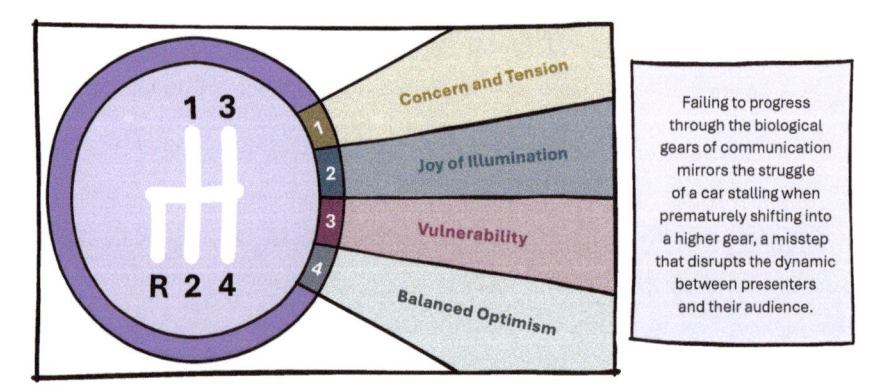

Figure 8.3: There should be a natural flow between presenter and audience.

The situation of prematurely advancing to the "goodies" in your message opportunity is very real. And the solution to this problem of pivoting quickly to promoting your services or product innovation requires more than a casual effort. This challenge stems from the psychology of not only persuading the mindset of your audience but also transforming your own approach to storytelling. So, buckle up in that 6-point harness racing seat belt because we're about to hammer the accelerator and speed out of the pit lane.

Audience-First Thinking

A chance airport encounter with Neil Rackham's *SPIN Selling* in the early 1990s planted a seed that would later bloom in unexpected ways. As a young national sales manager devouring business books at Indy 500 speeds, Rackham's systematic approach to sales questioning and buyer values impressed me. While life raced on—family expansions, global career moves, and the realization that my golf skills wouldn't put food on the table—that seed lay dormant but alive.

Fast forward to 2005. My newly launched storytelling agency, Presentation Partners, faced a persistent challenge: presenters acknowledging their audience's importance but struggling to actually put audience needs first. Our clients had the desire to change. What they needed were practical mechanisms to transform that desire into action.

This need led us to develop the *Neuroscience of Persuasion*^{SM} framework. But one piece was absent—a tool for deep audience understanding. Here, that dormant SPIN seed sprouted. While Rackham's specific sales model wasn't the perfect fit for our work, it helped inspire our approach to audience analysis.

The answer would come from an unexpected place—my home library. Over years of marriage, my wife and I have filled our home with books—her novels transporting her to other worlds, while my shelves overflow with golf stories, rocket ships, and business science. As our collection grew unwieldy, Marie Kondo's *The Life-Changing*

Magic of Tidying Up taught us the joy of passing books on to spark joy in others' lives.

To spark joy for our clients, I was on a quest for the perfect tool to enhance audience understanding. I'm grateful I held onto Neil Rackham's *SPIN Selling*. As I pondered this challenge one day, the book seemed to wave at me from the shelf, inviting a closer look. Originally tailored for the sales-buyer relationship, its process encourages a gradual, time-based conversation between these two parties. However, our clients weren't always in a buyer-seller relationship, so we transformed the spirit of these ideas into something beyond pure sales. If done right, we could help a wider variety of clients visualize their assumed audience with an emotional snapshot of the various components of their specific world. This would extend beyond sales into the realm of broader business environments regarding communication. Rackham's model was an inspiration that led us to create something of our own that targets the EQ aspects of one's audience. This dovetailed nicely into our broader *Neuroscience of Persuasion*^{SM} framework for creating better narratives through storytelling. This was a step in the right direction, but it wasn't the complete solution.

Evolving the Model

While the SPIN approach excelled at the endurance race of long-term sales relationships, our clients were queuing for a drag race—one shot, full throttle, no pit stops. We needed to capture those same deep audience insights before the starting flag dropped. The solution emerged when we coupled our proprietary *Emotion Map* with a reimagined version of SPIN's principles, creating a tool that shocked our clients with a revelation: *My audience has an emotional posture ... who knew?*

Earlier in this chapter, we mentioned a few studies that focused on the attention of the audience. One of the summary statements offered was "Whatever is grabbing the attention of the audience, it is likely not you." I've always enjoyed reading that statement and sharing this in my talks. The term "grabbing" follows the idea of attracting attention. If the presenter stands on their head or shares a clever unknown story, they'll surely garner audience attention. Sustaining that attention is completely different. Most of us are not gifted orators; thus, we need other ways to sustain attention. The surefire way to sustain attention is the entire point of this chapter. Make it about capturing an emotive snapshot of your audience. If you desire a robust chance of sustaining their capture, then what you deliver must be meaningful in addition to making it about them. And if you fail to make it about your audience, you've just become another provider with an indistinguishable solution.

Learning from Failure

Even our storytelling agency can pull the wrong club out of the golf bag. Case in point: Do you remember the 2010 Deepwater Horizon oil spill? This was a catastrophic environmental disaster in the Gulf of Mexico, where an offshore drilling rig explosion released approximately 4.9 million barrels of crude oil into the ocean over 87 days. The spill, one of the largest in history, is responsible for the loss of 11 lives and caused extensive damage to marine and wildlife habitats as well as the regional fishing and tourism industries.

One of our clients offered a potential solution to the massive oil cleanup, and their audience was none other than the president of the United States. Given the urgency and the highly technical nature of the solution, we shifted straight into second gear to simplify the message. Unfortunately, in our haste to skip first gear, we neglected our usual process of delving into the audience's perspective, which we believe ultimately hurt our clients' pitch and their opportunity to be chosen. We got caught up in the situation and the two-day turnaround demanded by the project. What I should have done was step back and spend 50% of the prep time, in this case one entire day, focused on what the POTUS must have been dealing with in this highly visible and complex situation. To this day, it saddens me to think that we missed an opportunity to contribute to a significant environmental cleanup effort at this scale.

This experience underscored the importance of understanding the audience, a lesson that has proven invaluable in our work with various clients over the years. Observing and documenting the emotional and intellectual snapshots of their audiences has been a fascinating process, revealing insights that might otherwise go unnoticed. Overlook this, which is easily done when you spend 90% of your time on the solution, and there's a high probability that no matter how well you craft a great narrative, it's the wrong one. It manifests itself in the aftershock of "How did we lose this?" or "We didn't see this one coming."

The Professional's Approach

Just as elite golfers study the course's character—its terrain, grasses, winds, and hazards—long before teeing off, dealmakers who master a pillar of the *Neuroscience of Persuasion*[SM] understand their audience's emotional landscape before crafting their pitch. While your competition obsesses over their own capabilities—like an amateur golfer overthinking their swing mechanics during a crucial round—you'll gain the advantage by first reading the deeper conditions: your audience's fears, aspirations, and unspoken needs. No amount of technical skill can overcome poor course awareness in golf; similarly, even the most innovative solution falls flat when presented without understanding the emotional terrain you're playing on. The amateur fixates on their swing while the pro stays attuned to the course; likewise, while your competitors focus on features and benefits, you'll be mapping the emotional contours that truly drive decisions. This is what separates those who simply participate from those who consistently win.

9

Pure Message Moonshine

Distilling Content to Meaning

In the early days, our agency's early battle cry was a playful twist on Patrick Henry's famous words: "Give me clarity or give me death by *PowerPoint!*" While Henry's plea was a matter of life and death, our lighthearted version illuminates the peril of dull presentations. You know exactly how this feels because you've either sat in the audience watching a presenter ramble on or, sadly, watched your team member do the same thing. In either case, it is astonishing that someone can speak for 15 minutes straight and say absolutely nothing of value. Let's be clear: Crafting a meaningful message is impossible if it's all about your solution and ignores the audience.

Our previous topic on the forgotten audience, when combined with intense focus, can spark a desire to ensure your listeners or readers receive something truly meaningful. So, only once you know the point of view of your audience can you distill your persuasive argument to meaning. Think of this distillation the same way the spirits industry values concentration, purity, flavor, and shelf life. Master distillers know their consumers before they touch their stills; successful storytellers know their audience's emotional quotient before they distill their message.

Audience members spend their days, as we all do, overwhelmed by complexity, so the last thing their brains want is more context-divorced facts to process or complex terminology to parse[16]. This is the theory in a peer-reviewed study led by Fortenbaugh that suggests that while

---

[16] Fortenbaugh, F. C., J. DeGutis, and M. Esterman, "Recent Theoretical, Neural, and Clinical Advances in Sustained Attention Research," *Annals of the New York Academy of Sciences* 1396(1) (2017):70–91. DOI: 10.1111/nyas.13318.

our ability to pay attention doesn't decrease, there is a growing mental cost to staying focused on one task for a long time. The longer we focus on a task, the more mentally strained we become. It is this feeling that routinely thwarts an audience from wanting to use up brain capacity listening to an over-indexed, boring presentation.

Keeping Your Audience in the Fairway

In the studious world of scholarly research, Lemke and Besser introduced an intriguing concept for the Wolters Kluwer Corporation by analyzing listening effort. To make their findings more relatable, let's frame their work through the lens of golf: *processing effort* is like the mental resources you swing at each task, while *perceived effort* is how heavy that club feels when you're standing on the 18th tee after hiking nearly five miles with a 13-pound bag, searching for lost balls in thick woods, and navigating endless hills through 17 grueling holes.

Each hole in golf demands a singular focus—one shot, one target at a time—also each slide in your presentation should carry one clear message. Imagine you and your team presenting to a room full of executives about rolling out an enterprise-wide software platform across four continents. Every slide is like a new hole on the course, requiring target awareness and precise execution.

The moment your presentation veers from the fairway into the rough, forcing your audience to hack through technical jargon to find clarity, they're no longer cruising along with you. Their processing effort spikes as they struggle to follow, and the *perceived effort* becomes overwhelming, causing them to disengage. **When audiences wrestle with granular intricacies, they've lost sight of your larger story.**

The golfer's goal is to complete 18 holes in as few strokes as possible, and your pitch goal should be the

> When audiences wrestle with granular intricacies, they've lost sight of your larger story.

same—delivering a message with minimal thoughts. Keep your audience in the fairway by maintaining a clear communication arc—one thought per slide, no diversions into the woods of multiple competing ideas. This approach ensures they remain attentive and fully absorb the high-level story of even the most complex topics.[17]

The Pressure to Prove Intelligence

You might wonder why presentations often convey messages in such a complex manner. A prevailing theory suggests that this complexity stems from our deep-seated desire to show intelligence. This drive to prove our smarts isn't random. From an early age, our educational system rewards us with grades, tracking GPAs and certifications, reinforcing this behavior. This pursuit of recognition continues into our professional careers through performance-based promotions, salary increases, and peer accolades. From childhood through our careers, businesspeople grow accustomed to proving their smartness. The pressure to appear knowledgeable is substantial, driving us to pack our presentations with extensive content to showcase our expertise.

As a professional, you're under pressure to show vast knowledge. This can lead to presentations being overloaded with detail. While demonstrating expertise or perceived value is often critical, it can also send the communicator down an undesirable rabbit hole. The secret sauce in crafting meaningful messages is crafting thoughtful, crystal-clear solutions served up easier than a 1-foot putt on the 18th hole. But let's not confuse this with mere clarity. I learned this the hard way back in my *Neuroscience of Persuasion*[SM] research days—I was leaning toward the idea that one of the main pillars was all about *clarity*

---

[17] Lemke, U., and J. Besser, "Cognitive Load and Listening Effort: Concepts and Age-Related Considerations," *Ear and Hearing* 37, Suppl. 1 (2016):77S–84S. DOI: 10.1097/AUD.0000000000000304.

until being successfully persuaded that a message could be as clear as a cloudless sky but deliver no substance to the audience. To this day, it was an argument that I am glad I lost.

It may sound simple to deliver a meaningful message, but it's the hardest part of an excellent presentation. By having an existing command of our content, presenters cannot resist a deep dive into IQ-based facts with extensive validation of the greatness of their offer. They will typically overamplify the shininess of their solution, believing that by making their point repeatedly, the more the audience will simply succumb. Let's go to the practice range and get warmed up before we play the golf course, so we can put the idea of amplifying your value to the client to bed once and for all.

Meaningful Impact for Your Audience

It is worth recalling a couple of key points from Chapter 5, Your Brain's Factory Settings, where we identified important considerations about our audiences. These points are essential as we refine how to hone a meaningful message. The observations made by scientists Alan Jasanoff, Daniel Plebanek, and Vladimir Sloutsky underscore this:

> **Our audiences do not possess secret supercomputers in their heads.**
>
> **+**
>
> **Humans often seek cognitive shortcuts or simpler solutions when faced with complex tasks.**

In crafting deeply meaningful and clear content for our audience, it is crucial to heed the observations laid out by scientific insights into human cognition. The aforementioned three scientists provide pivotal insights that can derail a message's impact if overlooked. Their research underscores two critical tendencies: first, that our audiences' brains lack the processing power of supercomputers, demanding that we avoid overloading them with excessive detail. This means we need to stop adding layers of complexity to our message, attempting to make it more impressive. Second, the human propensity to seek cognitive shortcuts suggests our presentations must anticipate and accommodate this need for simplicity. There is perhaps no more fitting description that underscores this than Mark Twain's infamous quote: "I apologize for the long letter, but I didn't have time to write a short one." It is not just about being brief; it's about being impactful.

Too often, the urge to speed through content development, eager to deliver all the "goodies," results in slides crammed with intricate details—like an eager Formula 1 driver who, in his pursuit of the fastest lap time possible, negates the degrading care of his tires, ultimately losing significantly more race positions to competitors because he wore his tires out too quickly. **Overloading presentations with details creates a *distraction of intricacies*, sucking the audience away from grasping a meaningful message.**

Imagine the precision required by a professional golfer, where the outright power of their swing must be controlled meticulously, not to just reach the correct distance of the target but to accurately not disperse too far left or right of the target. Similarly, our story approach should be thoughtful to balance offering just the right amount of content—like how Goldilocks in the classic fairy tale preferred her porridge to be neither too hot nor too cold, but just right, and how your content must anticipate the audience's need for shortcuts.

> **Overloading presentations with details creates a *distraction of intricacies*, sucking the audience away from grasping a meaningful message.**

Narrative Versus Slide Content

Ultimately, a fair portion of the success of our presentations, narratives, and stories hinges on recognizing these cognitive limitations and instilling preferences into our meaningful message. Without this application of principles, we fail to create a pathway that guides the audience through the information landscape. This renders the audience unable to absorb and appreciate a meaningful message because the content is littered with *distractions of intricacies*. In presentation slide parlance, this is what it looks like:

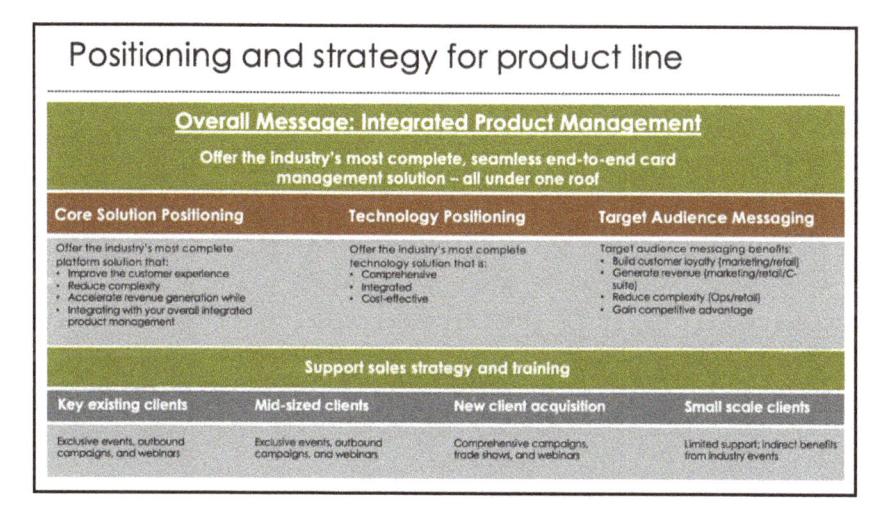

Figure 9.1: A challenging slide presents *distractions of intricacies*, where the audience loses focus of what the presenter is attempting to communicate.

Prioritizing Slide Content Over Narrative (Mistaken Approach)

This slide example is a crazy circus of distractions, a veritable feast for the eyes—if your eyes enjoy utter chaos. And remember, this beauty is just one of 25 similar disasters in the entire presentation deck. That's right, we're dealing with a multiplier effect here: imagine 25 times the chaos you see before you. With 176 words packed onto this single

Story: The Currency of Influence

slide, the total word count balloons to 4,400 across the entire presentation. That's 75% more words than you'd find in a typical Tom Clancy chapter. But let's be honest: Clancy's nuclear submarine dramas are infinitely more interesting than this snoozefest. Plus, he actually knows a thing or two about how to write. So, unless you have a secret career as a bestselling novelist, then let's soldier through because you're about to transition into the *how* of not being that presenter.

Words on a slide are a great measuring stick, but the impetus for distraction on a presentation slide begins with the number of thoughts the presenter is attempting to convey. It's like a golfer standing over a crucial shot while simultaneously thinking about keeping their head steady, maintaining grip pressure, making a full swing turn, rotating their hips to the target, keeping their left arm straight, and transferring their weight forward for the follow through—the result is almost always a chunk into the lake. Consider the next slide example: We've identified 6 independent thoughts hitting the audience all at once. Again, let us imagine this disparate content magnified by a factor of 25 to represent the entire slide count within a full presentation deck.

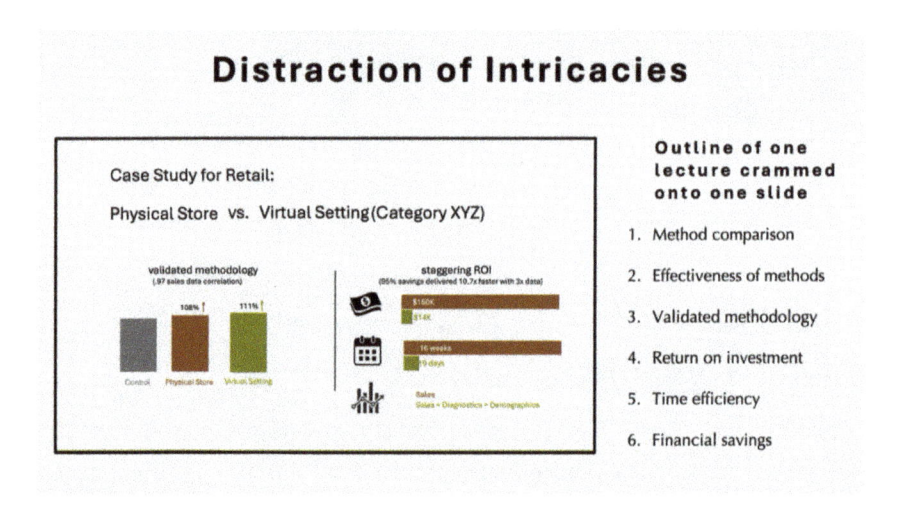

Figure 9.2: BEFORE: Too many disparate thoughts create a *distraction of intricacies* for the audience.

That's right—with 25 slides like this, the entire deck escalates to a whopping 150 independent thoughts that the beleaguered audience is supposed to stitch together in a coherent message. With these six thoughts all presented on one slide, you might mistake it for the outline of an entire lecture:

1. A comparison of methods
2. Effectiveness of methods
3. Validity of the methodology
4. Return on investment
5. Time efficiency
6. Financial savings

And yet, in fact, the presenter audaciously crams all these independent thoughts into just one slide of a presentation. Indeed, they do. It happens every single day by well-meaning business executives, deflating the efficacy of messaging and costing corporations' significant economics that we can't even tally. However, there is a better way forward. By focusing on meaningful messaging, we can transform these cluttered presentations into powerful narratives. That's why we've taken the previous presentation slide example and redeveloped it so that the primary focus is the narrative.

Prioritizing Narrative Over Slide Content (Correct Approach)

At first glance, you might consider this redeveloped slide in Figure 9.3 to be a better design—and it certainly is. Yet, the improvement isn't because of the design itself, but the result of a more meaningful message.

Story: The Currency of Influence

Clear Message, Clear Impact

Virtual store testing; outperforming reality.

87% LESS COST
SPEED TO SOLUTION 9x
3.5x MORE DATA

$28k / 10 days
$260K / 3 mo.

One central idea with clear metrics to support the idea

Figure 9.3: AFTER: Metrics serve one purpose—
to validate a resonant singular thought for your audience.

When business executives submit slide content to designers with too many thoughts and too many words, the designer becomes handcuffed, failing to deploy their artistic talents. By offering the design team "1" singular thought with a few validating metrics—like in Figure 9.3—they can work their visual magic because their sandbox to play in isn't crowded. Create slide content with white space and watch your designers flourish.

The reason this slide example in Figure 9.3 now works is because of the "1" singular thought that must be resonant with the audience: *the incredible performance of virtual store testing*. Every other piece of copy—and we must be careful here not to over-index—supports that "1" singular thought. Therefore, it is crucial to attack this problem head-on and address the myriads of thoughts. This is where our proprietary metric, the *Clarity Code*™—1–25–35, came into play. Let's pull the engine cover off the race car and examine some important ratios that create power and speed.

The *Clarity Code*™—A Single Resonant Thought

Figure 9.4: The *Clarity Code*™ 1–25–35.

Having too many thoughts on any presentation slide is like having 17 tabs open in your internet browser, with three of them frozen and unresponsive, leaving you puzzled about where a mysterious audio file is playing from. To halt this madness, start by pinpointing the single, crucial thought that needs to resonate with your audience. It can be as simple as asking yourself or the presenter, "What one point must the audience take away from this slide?" However, don't mistake simplification for generalization. Just as Formula 1 engineers make precise adjustments to specific aerodynamic parts rather than wholesale changes, you'll achieve better results by refining individual thoughts with surgical precision. This targeted approach keeps your message sharp while preserving its power to move your audience to action.

Story: The Currency of Influence

The Distraction of Intricacies in Action

Let us review the following before-and-after examples that illustrate the transformation from a content-focused slide to a narrative-driven presentation slide with an emphasis on *precision*. The BEFORE presentation slide in Figure 9.5 bombards the audience with so many thoughts that it's hard to grasp the meaning of the word "optimal" in the presenter's title. This slide messaging approach is such a broad swipe that the audience is stuck in the *distraction of intricacies*, diverting their attention from whatever the entrepreneur is trying to convey verbally.

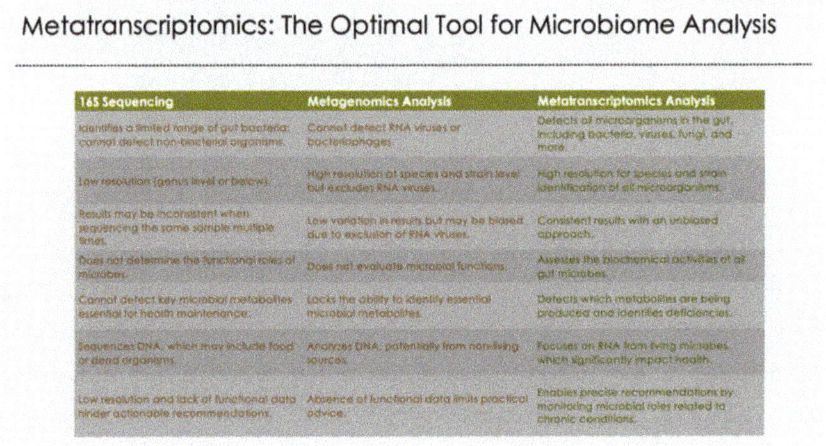

Figure 9.5: BEFORE: Presenter-centric content focused on demonstrating immense expertise, creates a *distraction of intricacies*.

By contrast, the presenter of the AFTER-presentation slide in Figure 9.6 understood that audiences care more about *why* something matters than *what* it does. They focused first on their narrative by clearly defining why their solution deserves attention: their process—metatranscriptome—is a game changer in the microbiome market, providing an almost infinite number of data points for diagnosis. By allowing the audience to deduce whether 150,000 data points offer more value than the nearest competitive process, which provides only 100 data points, you enable the audience to arrive quickly at the intended message on their own by simply presenting "1" singular thought on the slide.

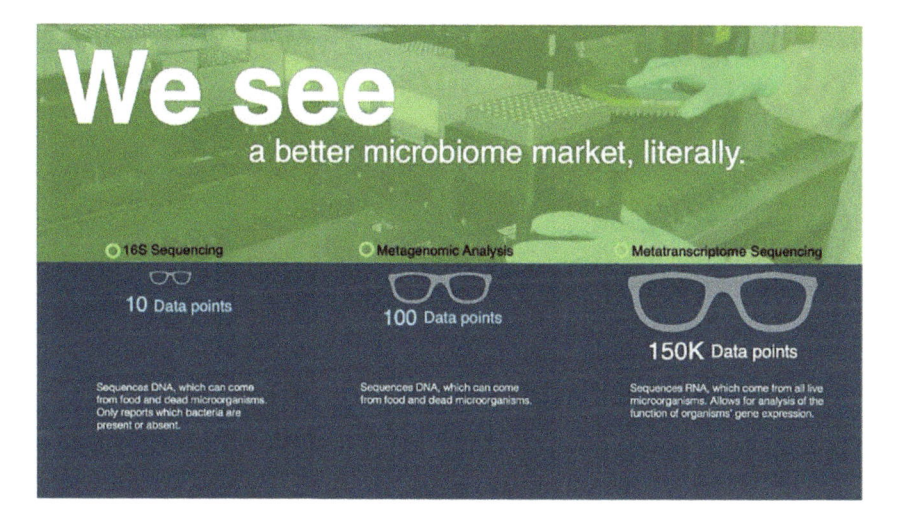

Figure 9.6: AFTER: Audience-centric slide driven by the narrative talk-track of the presenter, focusing on one clear thought for the slide.

Precision Targeting Rather than Carpet-Bombing

In reviewing close to a million slides, I've learned an essential truth: Each slide must convey a single, resonant thought. I can hear the skepticism now: "Too simplistic." "They won't take me seriously with just a headline." Fair concerns—if you stopped there. But that single thought is just your starting point. Follow it with another clear thought on the next slide, and another. And here's the key: Leave them wanting more. When they dig deeper with questions (and they will), you'll wow them with your preparedness with detailed appendix slides tailored for those rabbit-hole explorers. **Spreading fewer thoughts across more slides will enhance both clarity and delivery speed.** Counterintuitive as it may seem, more slides with fewer thoughts per slide speed up your

Story: The Currency of Influence

---

presentation while increasing clarity. Your audience stays engaged because they can digest each focused point, and you maintain control of your narrative while having the detailed backup ready when needed.

> **Spreading fewer thoughts across more slides will enhance both clarity and delivery speed.**

By focusing each slide on a single, resonant thought, you pave the way for the effective application of the *Clarity Code*'s second metric: word count. This focused approach simplifies keeping your slides concise, typically no more than 25 words.

The *Clarity Code*™—Fewer Words

Figure 9.7: The *Clarity Code*™ 1–25–35.

Just as we saw how multiple thoughts per slide create a cognitive traffic jam, trying to trim word count without first establishing one clear thought per slide is an exercise in futility. Think of slide design like preparing a car for a race. A slide crammed with 100+ words is like trying to race an RV with a satellite dish, while towing a boat—it might carry everything you think you need, but it's going to be painfully slow getting around the track. A slide with 50 words is like entering a Kia Soul in the race—better, but still not optimized for performance. The target of 25 words or less per slide is your race-ready Formula 1 car—stripped down to the essentials, aerodynamically efficient, and purpose-built for performance.

Without first focusing on one resonant thought per slide, hitting that 25-word target would be like trying to lighten that RV by removing a few cup holders—an exercise in futility. But when we control the ratio of one slide to one resonant thought, we achieve that perfect race trim. Just as a well-balanced race car performs efficiently through both tight corners and straightaways, a well-trimmed slide delivers its message with precision and impact. This methodical reduction in word count isn't just about aesthetics—it's about optimizing your presentation's performance, exactly as our scientific observations suggested.

The Split-Attention Effect

We've articulated scientific support for fewer words, lessening the cognitive load. Yet, another challenge exists that should appeal to your common sense. If you had to count backwards out loud from ten to one, you'd say "easy." Ratcheting this up, you're asked to say the alphabet backwards. Significantly harder, but doable with intense focus. The moment when you are asked to switch between the two, you're stopped dead in your tracks. This simple exercise demonstrates how our brain struggles when forced to process competing streams of information simultaneously, a challenge that plays out in presentations every day.

Presentation audience members can absorb content through two sensory channels: eyes and ears. However, there's a significant challenge in presentation development related to how audiences process information when they must split their attention between listening to the speaker and reading slides. Studies show that when we present audiences with too much information simultaneously across different mediums, such as spoken words and visual text, they struggle to absorb any of it effectively. Educational psychology calls this the *split-attention effect*.

This suggests that reducing *split-attention* by integrating auditory and visual information—such as a presenter's words with supportive slide content—can reduce cognitive load and enhance learning efficiency. No longer does the audience feel the need to answer unimportant emails on their phone or get a fourth cup of coffee during your presentation. Ideally, slides should visually summarize or reinforce the presenter's one resonant thought rather than introduce new, detailed text that competes for the audience's attention. This approach helps to reduce cognitive load by ensuring that both the auditory and visual information complement each other, facilitating easier information processing and retention. If possible, information sources should be restricted to a single entity.[18] We should focus on reducing cognitive load so the audience can skim the slide and then focus solely on listening to the presenter. **If there are too many words for the audience to read while listening, then you've crippled your voice.**

The goal is for each slide to be instantly understandable, ideally within seconds, much like viewing a billboard.

> **If there are too many words for the audience to read while listening, then you've crippled your voice.**

---

[18] Chandler, Paul and John Sweller, "Cognitive Load Theory and the Format of Instruction," *Cognition and Instruction* 8, no. 4 (1991): 293–332, DOI: 10.1207/s1532690xci0804_2.

Pure Message Moonshine

Figure 9.8: We all inherently know that too many words kill the vibe.

Audience Engagement: The 80/20 Rule

Using 25 words per slide—implementing the 80/20 rule that targets 80% listening and 20% reading—effectively prevents the split-attention effect. This structure supports our *Clarity Code*'s 35-second talk-track, allocating approximately 7 seconds for slide reading.

Slide Content to Prevent Split-Attention Effect

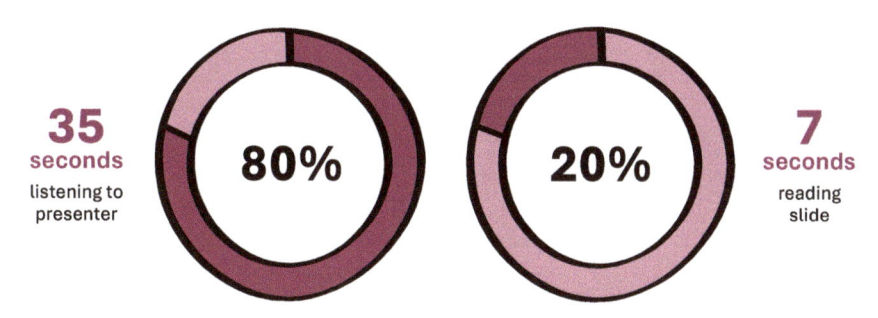

35 seconds listening to presenter — **80%** | **20%** — **7 seconds** reading slide

Figure 9.9: Using over 25 words per slide disrupts the 80/20 rule, tipping the split-attention effect against you.

Story: The Currency of Influence

Try this quick experiment: While reading this next paragraph, count backward from 100 by sevens. You'll quickly discover why we insist on the 25-word limit. Even this simple multitasking shows how your brain struggles to process competing inputs simultaneously. Now imagine your audience trying to read Frankenstein slides while also following your crucial message about quarterly projections or strategic transformations.

It's crucial to remember that realistically, audiences absorb about 80% of what they hear—not 100%, as one might assume. Nonetheless, in the storytelling agency business, less is more. Without fail, if you push beyond 25 words per slide, the magic begins to fade.

Consider the visual approach shown in Figure 9.10, which you've probably used throughout your career when building presentation slides. It's not entirely your fault; after all, most of us were never formally taught how to structure slide content. We mimicked what was likely first seen in school, where teachers or professors presented coursework using slides, and then carried this style into the business world. Despite any nagging feelings that this type of slide construction was not doing any favors for the soon-to-be tortured audience, it became the norm. It looked something like this:

The Traditional Slide

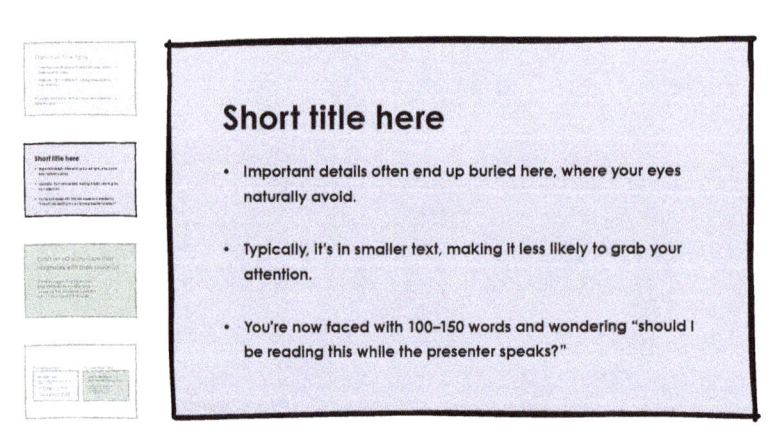

Figure 9.10: This example illustrates the pitfalls of traditional slide design—crucial information is often buried in dense, hard-to-read text at inconvenient places on the slide.

Pure Message Moonshine

The problems with traditional slides go beyond just challenging content delivery. Most presenters create short titles that simply remind themselves what topic they're covering, rather than crafting headlines that communicate clear value to their audience. Using the *Clarity Code*™ and our understanding of EQ, we can transform these weak titles into more engaging slides that look like this:

The *Clarity Code*™ Slide

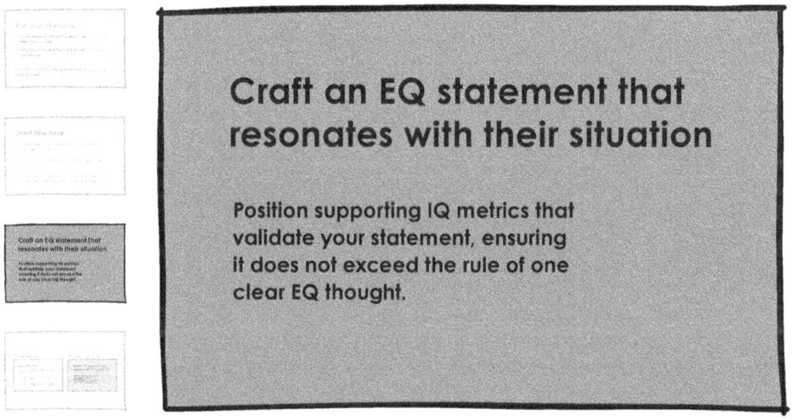

Craft an EQ statement that resonates with their situation

Position supporting IQ metrics that validate your statement, ensuring it does not exceed the rule of one clear EQ thought.

Figure 9.11: By striving for one clear thought, achieving just 25 words per slide becomes a more achievable target, making it easier for the reader to absorb content.

Don't Trust Your Eyes

Upon completion of a document or presentation slide, don't just casually review with your eyes; counting words matters. Check with your favorite novelists; they'll likely go as far as counting syllables, aiming to lighten their readers' cognitive load. A great example of word-persnicketiness is Warby Parker, a company that's mastered the art of brevity. With every pair of glasses sold, they include a lens cleaning cloth that narrates their entire company history in less than 100 words. Now, that's making every word count!

Story: The Currency of Influence

Warby Parker in Less Than 100 Words

Once upon a time, a young man left his glasses on an airplane. He tried to buy new glasses. But new glasses were expensive. "Why is it so hard to buy stylish glasses without spending a fortune on them?" he wondered. He returned to school and told his friends. "We should start a company to sell amazing glasses for non-insane prices," said one. "We should make shopping for glasses fun," said another. "We should distribute a pair of glasses to someone in need for every pair sold," said a third. Eureka! Warby Parker was born.

Figure 9.12: Warby Parker's company history condensed into less than 100 words, demonstrating the power of succinct EQ storytelling instead of detailed IQ narratives.

To give you a clearer picture, let's rewind to a slide we dissected earlier in Figure 9.1. In this example, a presenter attempted to explain a bankcard platform service using a dizzying 174 words—all crammed onto a single slide. And, ahem, there were 24 more slides to accompany this. Frankly, it was a masterclass in how not to engage an audience. And if we're honest, that slide likely lost its audience faster than a bewildered tourist in Times Square.

Now contrast that with Warby Parker's precise brevity. They encapsulated their entire company history in less than 100 words on a humble lens cloth—and they did it so effectively that it not only informed me but also truly engaged me. First, they connected emotionally, tapping into the universal angst of losing something valuable.

Pure Message Moonshine

Then, they highlighted the pragmatic pain of overpaying for essentials like eyeglasses. And finally, they transformed a simple transaction into a fun adventure and a charitable act. This elevated the customer experience, and they did it in less time than you'd spend waiting for your microwave popcorn to pop.

While I've sat through countless pitches in my career, few have left an impression as lasting as those succinct words from Warby Parker. For now, let's shift our focus to the third element of the *Clarity Code*™: narrative precision.

The *Clarity Code*™—Narrative Precision

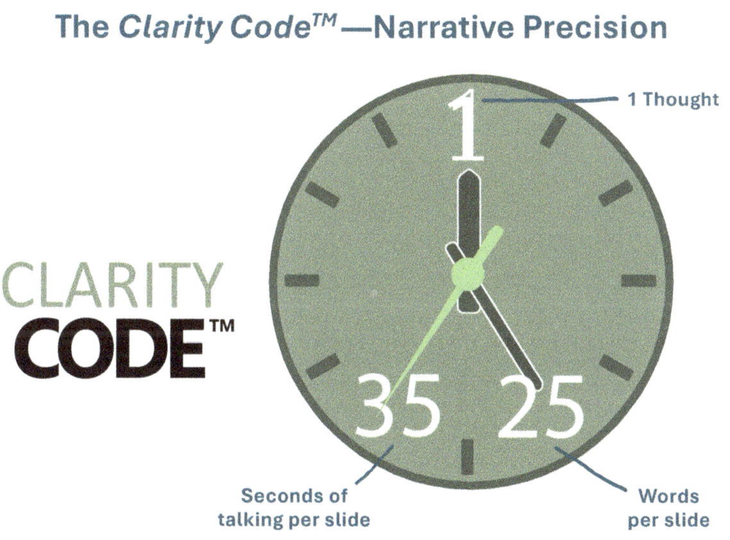

Figure 9.13: The *Clarity Code*™ 1–25–35.

I have a friend and associate who was a well-known national sports anchor. He has an incredible gift for word proficiency, which is common in his profession. They can comfortably speak around 250 words per minute, just as auctioneers can speak upward of 400 words per minute. For us mere mortals who are called upon to be presenters, the National Center for Voice and Speech (NCVS) states that a more realistic pace is about 150 words per minute.

Story: The Currency of Influence

word proficiency per minute

Auctioneer 400
Media Anchor 250
Biz People 150

Figure 9.14: Professionals speak at different paces. Realizing the speaking rate of business professionals and the diminished attention span gives us a finite number of words to engage audiences.

The Precision Mathematics of Engagement

Because of our human desire to impress others, our tendency is to go long—what I refer to as "circling the control tower" but not landing the plane. This is common for all of us, me included, and we just keep on talking and looking for a safe runway to land on. Research shows that the average adult's attention span wanes after about 10 minutes of listening.[19] Based on the average speaking pace of 150 words and the 10 minutes before adult attention wanes, the presenter has 1,500 words at their disposal to actively engage their audience. Imagine on your next flight, before descending, the pilot begins an announcement stating they've forgotten whether the destination is Denver or Dallas. However, the agitated passengers would quickly remind him. Yet, this is what so many of us do when speaking to a group of businesspeople.

---

[19] Bradbury, N. A., "Attention Span During Lectures: 8 Seconds, 10 Minutes, or More?" *Advances in Physiological Education* 40, no. 4 (2016) 509–513. DOI: 10.1152/advan.00109.2016.

Pure Message Moonshine

Takeoff, fly, then fail to land the plane in a timely fashion because we forgot where we were going. The challenge becomes—especially if presented with a slide deck—how to parse out and manage those 1,500 words before the 10 minutes expire.

The *Clarity Code*™ provides the precision framework to prevent us from circling that proverbial control tower. Let's break down the math in simple terms: With 10 minutes before attention wanes and an average speaking pace of 150 words per minute, we have exactly 1,500 words to work with. Through years of testing, we've found that 80 words per thought aligns with how humans optimally process information. At our 150 words/minute pace, this translates to our magic number: 35 seconds per slide (80 words ÷ 150 words per minute × 60 seconds = 32–35 seconds). This timing allows us to deliver approximately 17 resonant thoughts (10 minutes divided into 35-second segments) before attention spans drift. Just as a Formula 1 driver has precise calculations for car balance, battery usage, and fuel consumption, these numbers give us the framework for a successful presentation "race plan." For now, let's concentrate on crafting one of these resonant thoughts that can captivate an audience in just 35 seconds.

What does a 35-second talk-track for one presentation slide look like? For illustrative purposes, we will examine a slide from one of our earliest long-standing customers that supplied the aviation industry with maintenance planning software. The slide begins with a clear singular idea: There are "factors obscuring this strategic opportunity." The narrative articulates this through a concise talk-track crafted from three targeted sentences, each reinforcing this central theme, keeping within 80 words to maintain our suggested 35-second talk-track.

Story: The Currency of Influence

Putting the Code into Practice

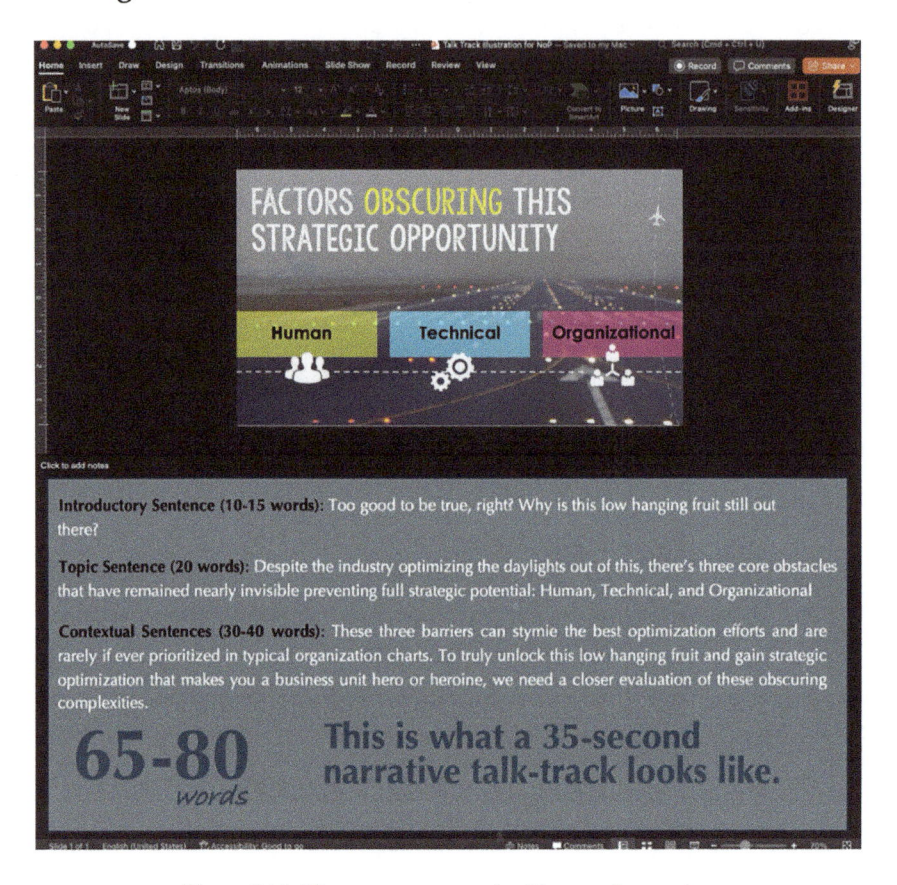

Figure 9.15: The secret to a concise 35-second narrative talk-track is to create structure to prevent verbose rambling.

It's almost unheard of that a business presenter could explain any slide and entice a listener in just 35 seconds. However, following this intentional structure, it works well as a talk-track, as we have outlined in Figure 9.15. As Confucius famously remarked, "Silence is a true friend who never betrays." This suggests that sometimes, saying less can be more impactful and engender trust. This insight underscores the impact of simplicity within communication, emphasizing that effective messaging hinges more on substance than volume. If there's one takeaway from crafting *meaningful messages,* it is the underlying message that brute force or mere amplification of a narrative cannot transform existing content into something meaningful.

Consider starting from scratch with a sense of precision. Race car drivers can thread their cars within centimeters of walls at incredible speeds. But they didn't start by practicing next to concrete barriers. They mastered their skills on open courses first, where mistakes wouldn't end in disaster. Only then could they execute with precision at high speeds near walls. Your path to masterful storytelling should follow the same principle—perfect your techniques in low-stakes environments before taking them into your next critical presentation. In the story world, to find a meaningful message, you'll need to get away from a slide full of distractions.

The same principle applies to your story content on presentation slides. You can't create clear meaning while wrestling with a complex, cluttered slide. Just as race car drivers perfect their skills on open courses before tackling wall-lined circuits, you need to step back from your *distractions of intricacies*—those dense slides packed with multiple thoughts and excessive words. Start with simplicity: one clear thought, carefully crafted. Trying to forge clarity from complexity is like trying to learn race craft at the high-speed concrete canyons of the Indianapolis Motor Speedway or through Monaco's barrier-lined narrow streets—a near-impossible path to a positive outcome. As *Brain Rules* author John Medina boldly directed: "Burn your current PowerPoint presentations and make new ones." Now, through the *Neuroscience of Persuasion*[SM], you'll learn exactly how to create those new ones that truly connect.

Your Path to Meaningful Messages

That is why we've laid forth a path for you to hyperfocus on the creation of a singular resonant thought. We then guide you to craft a narrative of 65 to 80 words, which you can express to your audience in 35 seconds, paving the way to offer a condensed slide copy of 25 words or fewer per slide. This approach significantly reduces the cognitive load for your audience.

Delivering a meaningful message with clarity involves peeling away the layers of complexity and continually asking yourself what is truly meaningful for your audience until you get to the core essence. So, secure your safety tether because, like the Saturn V rocket poised on the launchpad, your presentation, fueled by clear and focused content, is ready to defy gravity and lift your audience to the moon.

10

The Science of Story

EQ Primacy

Why Metrics Aren't Your Star Player

"Emotional baloney?" That's what the occasional grizzled executive I've encountered over nearly two decades at our agency seems to scoff at. They often proclaim, "My client is a CFO of a Fortune 500 company; they don't want an emotional narrative." It always makes me chuckle when I hear this. I wonder if there's a sign at the entrance to a movie theater somewhere that reads, "Analytical CFOs Not Allowed!" Or "Beware, this movie theater contains emotional narratives." If the CFO is indeed a human, then emotional narratives are on the table, unless, of course, they're secretly equipped with a biological toggle switch that shuts off all emotion once they step into the boardroom—yeah, right.

Even the most data-driven minds appreciate a good yarn—they just prefer it quick, backed by solid evidence and clear logic. As with any personality profiling, someone's analytical nature is just a slice of their personality pie, not the whole dessert. As someone who enjoys diving into an excellent set of nerdy metrics, I understand their value in a story, but let's be clear: they're supporting actors, not the stars. So, when do analytics and metrics step onto the stage of a compelling narrative? Only *after* you've emotively engaged and captured your audience.

This is a significant claim because most business content and communication do the exact opposite. How do we know? Despite the internet's vast reach and endless guides on crafting better presentations, our agency hasn't experienced a downturn in companies needing help to make their content more engaging and meaningful over the last two decades. It seems advice is as common as the sport of football, yet the discipline of merging data with engaging narratives is as challenging as getting tickets to the Super Bowl.

The Emotional Gut Punch

A dynamic narrative makes it stick. This has been the way since the beginning of man. Incredible narratives have made books like Miguel de Cervantes's *Don Quixote* or Homer's *The Iliad* and *The Odyssey* survive the test of time. As an industry, Hollywood also benefits from spinning a good yarn. And, of course, corporations have been investing in storytelling for the last several decades, attempting to tap into the possibilities of stories. Spreadsheets and bullet points only came along much later in the game. Even with those, if we surround that sterile content with a sticky narrative, it carries more meaning for our audience. **When a fact is wrapped in a story, it is 7 to 10 times more memorable.**[20][21] That explains why major companies, from 3M to Nike, have significant corporate initiatives related to storytelling. A powerful story coupled with meaningful visuals captures attention and ensures that your audience remembers you.

To illustrate this power, let me indulge my nerdy obsession with the Saturn V rocket again—bear with me as I dive back into the marvel that I cannot resist. Consider the movie *Apollo 13*, based on the book *Lost Moon* by astronaut James Lovell. I read this book, which carried a technical heft appealing to nerds like me but not likely to the general public. The film, however,

> When a fact is wrapped in a story, it is 7 to 10 times more memorable.

---

[20] Heath, Chip, and Dan Heath, *Made to Stick* (Arrow Books, 2008).
[21] Bower, G. H., and M. C. Clark, "Narrative Stories as Mediators for Serial Learning," *Pschonomic Science* 14 (1969): 181–182. doi.org/10.3758/BF03332778.

masterfully tells the story of NASA's harrowing mission, transforming complex technical challenges into an engaging narrative that captivated audiences worldwide. The filmmakers took intricate details and wove them into a story that highlighted human ingenuity, teamwork, and perseverance. As a result, the movie didn't just inform viewers about the historical event, it made the story unforgettable. In the same way, incorporating a dynamic narrative into your presentations can elevate your content from mere information to a memorable experience, ensuring your message resonates long after the audience leaves the room.

Now, chances are your narrative isn't as dynamically interesting as the movie *Apollo 13*, but remember, the story began with an incredibly detailed (and historically important) book. And we can learn from movies how elements like structure, conflict, and resolution can shape a more dynamically memorable narrative.

In the movie *Apollo 13*, numerous scenes emotionally engage the audience with the plight of the three astronauts. Just when it seems every conceivable life-threatening obstacle reached a satisfying outcome, another issue emerges, threatening their safe return. As they approach the reentry corridor of Earth's atmosphere, NASA's Houston control center discovers the crew's trajectory is critically off because of a gross miscalculation from the absence of several hundred pounds of moon rocks, which weren't collected due to the mission's failure. The astronauts, seemingly moments from safety, now face an even greater risk of disaster and death, delivering a metaphorical gut punch to the audience, who thought the crew was finally home free.

While your presentation stakes may not be life-or-death, it should have moments of emotional impact—what we call gut punches. Our structured EQ audience snapshot methodology helps identify these key emotional moments for your audience. Like the scriptwriters for *Apollo 13*'s dramatic climax, you can harness similar emotional inspiration to create lasting connections that your competition never dreamed of. While mastering this approach requires deeper training beyond the scope of this book, in the next three segments we'll show you key principles you can begin applying immediately to your storytelling, keeping your audience fully engaged and your competition in the rearview mirror.

Why Your Logical Approach Isn't Working

Most business executives have been told at one time to start with a "problem statement." By beginning with a problem statement and a quickly followed solution, the audience will be interested. And they might be just a little, but usually not at the level you'd desire. Then you wonder why your audiences stare blankly from their frontcourt seats and miss the apparent slam dunk.

As dealmakers realize that their easy win opportunity isn't winning audiences over, our claim gains merit that analytics and metrics are best introduced after the emotional investment of the audience. If this holds true, it suggests a need for the business community to rethink their content-structuring strategies, especially if their goal is to ethically persuade someone to adopt their perspective. This shift would prioritize establishing an emotional connection *before* presenting hard data, aligning the presentation more closely with human cognitive and emotional processing patterns. However, beyond the appeal of critical reasoning, let's look at a few scientific perspectives to support what seems logical.

The Nobel Prize That Changed Business Storytelling

Fortunately, we have Susan Scott, the author of *Fierce Conversations* (an excellent read), who highlighted the importance of Daniel Kahneman and the research behind his 2002 Nobel Prize for Economics. Kahneman, intriguingly a psychologist, not an economist, snagged this prestigious award from the global economics community. This is significant despite being a somewhat humorous crossover. A group of the most influential economists in the world offers the most influential prize in economics to a ... psychologist? This underscores the profound impact psychological insights have on economic theories. For you, the megadeal maker, this should confirm that your data and metrics have a secondary role to support a bigger idea. His groundbreaking work revealed that our decisions—even economic ones—are influenced more by emotion than by rational thought[22], emphasizing the primacy of emotional engagement in human interactions. This unexpected crossover points to the vital intersection between psychology and economics, particularly in understanding how emotional responses influence economic decisions. It's exactly why I chuckle to myself when the grizzled executive claims their C-suite client is void of emotional need.

By leveraging this knowledge, presenters can more effectively engage audiences, ensuring that emotional connection precedes the introduction of complex data or analytics. This strategy not only resonates more deeply with audiences but also exploits fundamental human behavior to enhance communication impact and persuasive power. Who knew a psychologist would teach a community of economists a thing or two about emotions?

Groundbreaking Neuroscience 101

Primed with the behavior of prioritizing emotion ahead of intellectual facts, we must pivot to one driver of that behavior. Antonio Damasio, author and professor, wrote a landmark publication in 1995

---

[22] "Daniel Kahneman—Prize Presentation," NobelPrize.org, Nobel Prize Outreach AB 2024, December 9, 2024, https://www.nobelprize.org/prizes/economic-sciences/2002/kahneman/prize-presentation.

called *Descartes' Error*. The title itself challenges one of history's most famous philosophical statements—"I think, therefore I am"—penned by French philosopher René Descartes. While generations of business leaders have embraced Descartes's celebration of pure reason, Damasio's research revealed a different truth: Emotions aren't the enemy of rational thought—they're essential to it. His work changed our understanding of how neural systems underpin memory, language, and consciousness.

What I found most enjoyable in reading and listening to Professor Damasio is that through his Brain and Creativity Institute, they have discovered a beautiful piece of who we are. There's a fair amount of material in existence pointing to certain personality traits, cultural indications, or social styles, but there's one absolute: **People emote in predictable ways.**[23] They originally thought that, for emotions, cross-cultural people would emit very different social emotions. Think of the analytical CFO in an Asian culture versus the visually minded CMO in an American culture. However, their research led Damasio to conclude: "The presence of sadness or joy is there with a uniformity that is strongly and beautifully human." Above all, nuanced approaches categorize us as certain types of people; when it comes to our emotions, we are all human. So, as a presenter, you'd do well to remember the connection to your human audience requires emotion, even if they are an analytical CFO!

> **People emote in predictable ways.**

Damasio's significant research in the '80s and '90s prompted the authoring of *Descartes' Error*, which came from a series of studies about patients who, sadly, had brain lesions. The lesions prevented or severely limited their emotional capacity. Interestingly, the patients had

---

[23] Pontin, Jason, "The Importance of Feelings," *MIT Technology Review* (June 17, 2014): https://www.technologyreview.com/2014/06/17/172310/the-importance-of-feelings/.

full rational capacity. When given a math problem or anything that required critical reasoning, logic, language, or memory, they could execute flawlessly. In fact, this condition might seem rather ideal, in that most of us have been told or mentored that "cooler heads" prevail. That more rational thinking and less emotional intrusion will allow us to see a more advantageous path forward. Not so fast—this purely rational paradise might seem like a wide-open fairway in golf, but there's often an unexpected bunker just over the crest waiting to challenge our approach.

Finding Data's Role

The prevalence of data-driven insights has tempted business leaders to use even more rational thinking that is available at our fingertips. And I agree, it should be used, however it might be a question of *how* it's used. For instance, consider the case of a tech company where the CEO was launching an innovative smart-home device. The innovation was driven through extensive data analytics that highlighted consumer demand for more integrated home technology. Confident in the data, the CEO centered the launch presentation around the vast amount of consumer research and technical specifications. A plethora of presentable IQs awaited the audiences.

However, despite the robust data backing the product, the initial market reception was lukewarm. The CEO, having been deeply involved in the product's development, felt a strong emotional connection to the innovation and saw it as a key to transforming everyday living. The initial product launch became data-heavy, leaving out the emotional connection. It was only after retooling the campaign to include stories of how the product had personally affected the development team and beta testers—illustrating the potential changes in daily routines and the emotional benefits of convenience and security—that the public's interest and excitement aligned with his own.

This example underscores the importance of balancing data-driven rationality with the emotional narratives that resonate on a human level. While data is crucial, it is the emotional connection that often transforms respect and acknowledgment into enthusiasm and action.

Antonio Damasio's pivotal research on patients lacking emotional capacity revealed a startling paradox. **Despite one's ability to think rationally, individuals consistently fail to choose the most advantageous actions for themselves.** Their lives spiraled out of control, leading to severe social incompatibility. They found it nearly impossible to hold down any job or maintain personal relationships. This wasn't because of a lack of intelligence or rational thinking; they were completely normal in those areas. However, their inability to process and respond to emotions left them adrift in situations that require the complementary emotional understandings that make critical reasoning effective. Without emotional insight, they couldn't prioritize or make sound decisions despite having ample intellectual capabilities. Damasio's findings underscored the critical role emotions play in decision-making and social functioning, particularly those associated with the frontal cortices. This illustrates that rationality alone is not the key to choosing advantageous actions. Yet, businesspeople routinely believe that communication should be void of emotive narratives when communicating with an analytic senior executive. Emotions provide the context and guidance, helping your C-suite audience to navigate the complexities of business interactions and choices.

> **Despite one's ability to think rationally, individuals consistently fail to choose the most advantageous actions for themselves.**

Damasio's research spotlights a truth that challenges today's technology-driven business world: Emotions aren't just important for everyday life—they're crucial for decision-making. His studies of patients with brain lesions revealed something remarkable: Despite having full rational capabilities, these individuals struggled to make advantageous decisions because they lacked emotional insight. This finding has massive implications for presentations and storytelling. Without emotional quotient (EQ), even the most logically sound presentations leave our brains searching for more, creating a disconnect as jarring as an avid race fan (like me) attending a poetry conference. The audience may understand every word, but they're unlikely to act. Damasio's work delivers a coherent message for business communicators: Embracing EQ isn't just beneficial—it's essential for moving people to action.

11

The EQ Sandwich™

Story: The Currency of Influence

Writing Mechanism, Inclusio

The EQ Sandwich™: A Structured Approach

What is the best sandwich you've ever eaten? For me, it's a marvelous three-part construction. There's something special about three parts, as opposed to just two—a gum-watering, scrumptiously layered BLT. Imagine thick slices of applewood bacon paired with crisp butter lettuce and vine-ripened tomato, all lovingly woven together with an herb and lemon mayonnaise. This delectable lunch took me on an emotional rollercoaster—first surprise, then utter joy, and then a smidge of sadness as the last bite vanished. That's the power of a good sandwich: It stirs up a symphony of emotions that leaves you craving more. The same is true for a well-crafted story; it surprises, delights, and leaves you longing for more.

Most business presenters that ignore the structure of a story fail to craft a complete message. In sandwich parlance, this is what it might look like. Just imagine my favorite BLT sandwich deconstructed. The server brought out just the bacon, perhaps with a small garnishment of butter lettuce on the side. I'd be disappointed—although, how disappointed could I really be in the presence of bacon? My stomach and my will disagree on this regularly. I might indulge anyway. While each element's taste is fine on its own, there's still a struggle to imagine something complete. However, I'm not craving more; in fact, I've had enough.

Now parallel this with the sandwich eater being the client, who sends out a request for bid to the market. The sandwich eater defined all the BLT's ingredients in unbelievable detail, as well as the process of food preparation. The sandwich eater dreamt of one potential partner putting all the ingredients into something magical. Instead, they got five bids describing their favorite ingredient separately: one detailed their smoking process for the bacon, another highlighted the nutritional qualities of the butter lettuce, and yet another was passionate about the terra firma where they grew heirloom tomatoes. This is a critical communication mistake made by countless teams pitching in the business world: While competent and differentiating from the other, each response misses an opportunity to weave these elements into something with a completely satisfying structure.

Your client, much like the sandwich eater, must deal with something that was less than the sum of its parts. The fortunate sandwich eater can just leave the restaurant table disappointed. Your client, on the other hand, does not have that luxury. They still must determine who to give the bid to: the tomato harvester raving about their terra firma or the lettuce farmer who's boasting of their organic credentials? Alas, they fall for the applewood smoked bacon—because when all else fails, who isn't pleased by the smell of really sumptuous bacon?

But what if we could transform this fragmented experience into something greater than its parts? The structure of the *EQ Sandwich*™ robustly combines philosophical insights, writing techniques for innate human behavior, and science. Crucially, its efficacy hinges on three fundamental parts. It's magical what three ingredients can turn into. Just some rye whiskey, bitters, and a little simple syrup, and you have an enjoyable cocktail. While Aristotle wasn't building a mixed drink, the great philosopher deconstructed our core topic of persuasion into three nearly magical elements[24]:

---

[24] Aristotle, *Nicomachean Ethics*, Translated by Roger Crisp (Cambridge University Press, 2014).

Story: The Currency of Influence

PATHOS
Emotional Appeal

ETHOS
Credibility

LOGOS
Logical Appeal

While Aristotle wasn't building a mixed drink, the great philosopher did deconstruct our core topic of persuasion into three nearly magical elements.

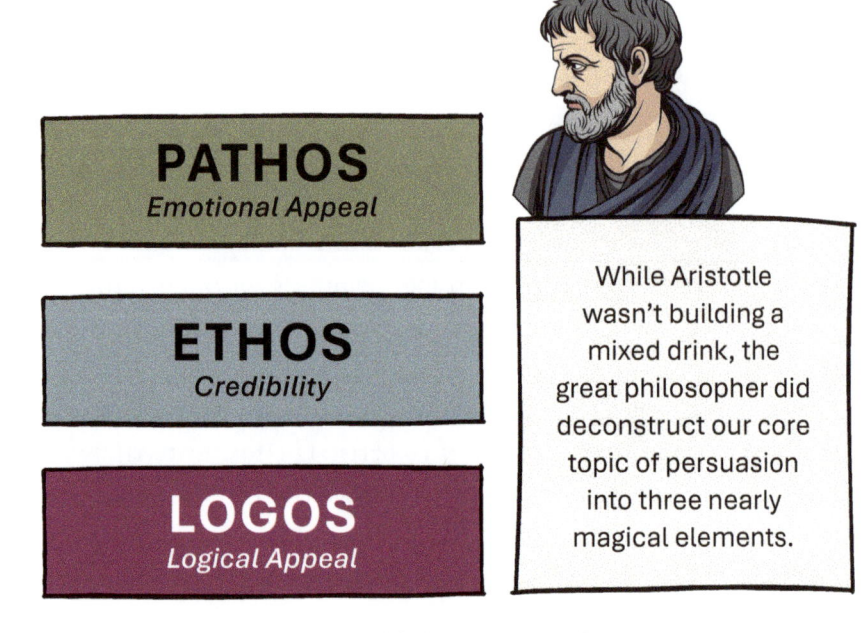

Figure 11.1: Aristotle's deconstruction of persuasion.

Twenty-plus centuries before, the emotional discoveries of psychologist Daniel Kahneman, the philosopher Aristotle, somehow knew that Pathos—the emotional appeal—was primary to win the influence of others. It's amazing and irrefutable that two brilliant minds spaced that far apart in history came to similar conclusions in their own respective ways.

The First Part of the Sandwich

With critical reasoning, the first fundamental part of a communication sandwich should begin by building a modern-day structure for businesspeople with Pathos on their minds. Using our own emotional quotient becomes the primary means to connect with people, even in the most complex business environments.

Like most kids growing up in the '70s I spent the occasional time plotting my escape routes from mom's liver nights at dinner. Mind you I had to be clever to escape this repeatedly. That said, I'm no scientist, and I'm certainly far from being a philosopher (unless pondering over the best pizza ingredients counts). However, I have over 35,000 hours of deliberate practice in the field of story construction, which, according to Malcolm Gladwell[25], should qualify as expertise—though I still have plenty to learn.

While I'm fully on board with Aristotle's first element of persuasion, I suggest that his next two—credibility and logical appeal—meld together like the herb and lemon mayonnaise and the vine-ripened heirloom tomatoes in the middle of a sandwich. Thus, we understand what makes up the reasoning for the middle of a three-layer sandwich.

The Second Part of the Sandwich

This second element, illustrated in Figure 11.1, is naturally one of the easier things for the modern businessperson to grasp; speaking in facts comes naturally. Credibility is one of those things that helps engender trust, a critical element in persuasion. **In the business environment, credibility demands proof—this is where your evidence and reputation unite to create trust.**

Logical appeal rests on demonstrating the validity of a company's solution, whether it's a service or a product. How well a presenter can logically validate their solution through previous successes is the path to show business credibility. Therefore, I believe that in modernity, these two elements—credibility and logical appeal—merge into

> **In the business environment, credibility demands proof— this is where your evidence and reputation unite to create trust.**

---

[25] Gladwell, Malcolm, *Outliers: The Story of Success* (Little, Brown and Company, 2008).

Story: The Currency of Influence

one stronger component in the middle of our tasty sandwich. Unless, of course, you prefer the "cross your fingers and hope for the best" strategy, which is always great for those who enjoy surprise career changes. But why not leave Aristotle's three elements as they were? As brilliant as he was, this is where modern-day science has essentially doubled down on the value of emotional appeal and shown how significantly humans are disadvantaged without emotion to help them make sound decisions.

The Third Part of the Sandwich

Modern science has made one thing crystal clear: Emotion isn't just important for decisions—it's the catalyst that drives people to act. This brings us to the third and final part of our sandwich, where we return to emotional appeal with even greater purpose. While we began with emotion to engage our audience and built credibility through the middle, we now harness it again to drive action. The findings of renowned neuroscientist Antonio Damasio proved this isn't just theory—it's biology. His research showed that individuals lacking emotional capacity face significant challenges in making beneficial decisions, while those with full emotional faculties are best reached through emotionally rich communication. Hence, failing to integrate emotional content that aligns with the natural inclinations of their brains would be a significant oversight. This emphasis on emotion not only completes our persuasive framework but also provides the psychological momentum needed to drive decisive action during the conclusion of a business pitch.

Aristotle's Persuasion Formula

- **PATHOS** — Emotional Appeal
- **ETHOS** — Credibility
- **LOGOS** — Logical Appeal

Modernity Path to Persuasion

- **PATHOS** — Emotional Appeal
- **ETHOS & LOGOS** — Credibility & Logical Appeal
- **PATHOS** — Emotional Appeal

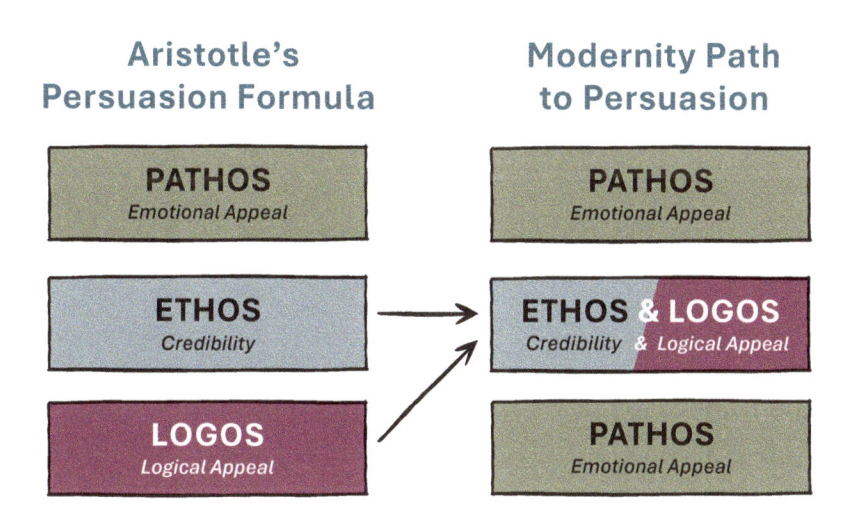

Figure 11.2: A reimagined persuasion model at the foundation of the *EQ Sandwich*™.

The Significance of Inclusio

There's one more significant reason a three-element communication piece instinctively meshes with humans. For centuries, literature resembled a sprawling golf course—vast and without clear markers guiding the way. That changed about 850 years ago when Archbishop Stephen Langton (c. 1150–1228) stepped up like a master caddie, neatly dividing the Bible into the chapters we use today. This reorganization was made workable by the ancient technique of *Inclusio*, where stories began and ended with similar themes, much like teeing off and putting on the green to complete a hole.

This literary approach didn't just give structure to the texts; it also emphasized key themes and helped navigate the narrative. This approach guided the listeners (and later the readers) to understanding the overall coherence and structure of the narrative, especially in oral traditions, where such cues were crucial for maintaining audience attention and conveying the message effectively.

The *Inclusio* technique reminds me of something someone once

Story: The Currency of Influence

told me about playing competitive rounds of golf: break the 18 holes into three mini-rounds of 6 holes each, where the first 6 holes and the last 6 holes matter the most. In golf this approach and prioritized focus made the entire round more manageable for optimal outcomes. Each segment of this three-part sandwich allows the executive to better manage what would otherwise be overwhelming, guiding one from the opening drive to the final putt, and ensuring capture of the story's full essence. This structure helps maintain attention and conveys messages in an era dominated by oral traditions. Now, with some critical reasoning behind this sandwich structure underscored, it's time to further explore how this model of the *EQ Sandwich*™ and its effective application for business professionals is worthwhile.

Words like Ethos and Pathos from ancient Greece and *Inclusio* from Latin might sound more like exotic menu items than tools for the modern businessperson. So, let's make it easier to digest with our *EQ Sandwich*™—a tasty alternative that won't just fill you up with empty-jargon calories. This is a hearty, nutritious framework you can sink your teeth into, perfect for energizing your next big phone call tomorrow or spicing up your pitch next week. No more snacking on outdated terms; it's time to feast on something that really satisfies your business appetite. And now, without further ado, let your server bring out the main course, complete with a drumroll …

EQ — Story
A red thread narrative makes it stick.

IQ — Meaning with Clarity
Give them clarity or give them death—by PowerPoint®.

EQ — Emotional Alignment
It's not about you. It's about them.

The EQ Sandwich™

Figure 11.3: EQ–IQ–EQ framework for storytelling that guides both verbal and visual words to deliver content the way humans best receive communication.

Imagine your business presentation as a journey through space, like the epic tale of *Apollo 13*. Each component of your story needs to orbit strategically around the central mission: making a lasting connection with your audience. Whether you're pitching technology services to clients or healthcare widgets to venture capitalists, the *EQ Sandwich*™ provides the perfect flight plan for your mission.

Like any good flight plan, the *EQ Sandwich*™ offers flexibility based on your mission parameters. The three components vary depending on the business context. For example, if you're pitching to a stodgy private equity firm during a series D capital raise, consider reducing the initial EQ–Emotional Alignment focus—but never eliminate it entirely, unless your audience is an alien from another planet. With a mature business that has gone through several rounds of capital raise, getting to the point quickly is key, so increase the IQ focus. Conversely, when engaging with an enterprise client where there is no formal bid or immediate opportunity, emphasize the EQ–Emotional Alignment phase and reduce the IQ section. This flexibility makes the *EQ Sandw*ich™ adaptable to any business scenario.

Think of it like this: sometimes you need a hearty Reuben, packed with emotional storytelling and layers of proof points for a skeptical audience. Other times, a chicken slider hits the spot—compact but complete, delivering just enough emotional connection to make the technical details digestible. And occasionally, you might need a triple-decker club sandwich when you're juggling multiple stakeholders with different appetites for data versus narrative. The beauty of the *EQ Sandwich*™ is that, like any great sandwich, it can be customized while maintaining its essential structure.

Storytelling Beyond the Realm of Slides

Structure matters tremendously to a good story, but the presenter matters more. Having this structure on a deck is great, but it needs to live

Story: The Currency of Influence

in your head—and the heads of your entire team. Your most powerful asset isn't the presentation story—it's how you apply this thinking to every communication touchpoint. The *EQ Sandwich*™ works at both the macro and micro levels—from structuring entire proposal documents to crafting individual responses to technical requirements.

Consider a complex RFP response where dozens of team members must answer hundreds of questions. Each response becomes a micro-sandwich—opening with an emotional connection to the client's needs, delivering the technical specifics, and closing with a reminder of the human impact. Or for that matter, you could serve an open-face sandwich, that begins with EQ followed by IQ, with no EQ at the close because you are word (or page) constrained in your response. As long as an emotional *why* initially sets the table, your communication structure is already enhanced. Meanwhile, the overall document maintains the macro-sandwich structure, with executive summaries that connect emotionally, technical sections that demonstrate capability, and conclusions that reinforce trust.

This nested approach acknowledges Kahneman's insight that emotion precedes rational thinking. Whether you're writing a one-line email or orchestrating a thousand-page proposal, just begin and end with EQ, and in the middle is your IQ sandbox. The beauty lies in its scalability—from boardroom presentations to bullet points, from keynote speeches to knowledge transfers. Have fun playing with this straightforward structure to create better stories, because ultimately, every business communication is an opportunity to make a human connection.

12

Threading Your Story Together

The Secret Sauce Is Red Thread

Using the structure of the *EQ Sandwich*™ for your important communications ensures you are delivering content in a way that resonates with human preferences, blending EQ and IQ elements effectively. Yet, I'd argue that being in pole position for the start of a Grand Prix doesn't mean you have a compelling story. When your story gets off the starting line slowly, you get passed. The accurate test of a great story is its memorability and the ease with which it can be passed on to others (on-communicate).

Consider the challenge of making typically dry business topics like generative AI or cybersecurity not only engaging but also uniquely memorable. Without memorability, your communication may be well-crafted, but it risks being just another well-aligned marketing piece that your audience forgets about in 30 minutes. Just like the way race car tires stick to the track, your story needs elements that cling to your audience's memory—inescapable and persistent, much like a gnat dive bombing your ear relentlessly on a patio on a summer evening. In the world of storytelling, you need something that will stitch everything together. You need a red thread.

The red thread is a universal symbol found in multiple mythologies. It represents guidance, destiny, and divine connection, illustrating how it weaves through the fates and stories of individuals across different cultures. In contemporary usage, particularly in storytelling and analytical contexts, the red thread refers to the underlying theme or narrative thread that connects various parts of a story or argument, ensuring coherence and understanding for the audience. This term is used to highlight how distinct elements of a story or presentation are linked to form a unified whole.

Threading Your Story Together

In crafting this book, which is considerably more extensive than a typical presentation or verbal pitch, I have woven several red threads throughout its narrative—themes of golf, race car driving, and astronautics. Importantly, none of these themes are the central subjects of the book. This illustrates a crucial aspect of using red threads effectively: they should serve as abstract, universally relatable metaphors that complement, rather than directly mirror, the chief topic. This strategy ensures that the themes resonate broadly with the cultural context of the audience, enhancing engagement and retention.

Here's a small example of red-thread concepts illustrated through an ordinal list. This list will highlight a variety of themes, showcasing their abstract and often indirect connection to the main topic:

RED THREAD	TOPIC	INDUSTRY
Chose your own adventure	Operational software	Global theme parks
Auto racing	Operational hardware & software	Commercial kitchens
Maritime navigation	Debt resolution	Fintech
The first automotive crossover	Business wear meets the gym	Casual clothing
The in crowd	Digital marketing	SMB Legal
A symphony in harmony	Backoffice transformation	Utilities

Figure 12.1: Red-thread themes are most effective in crafting compelling narratives when they draw from familiar and easily understood elements of our society.

A word of caution on spinning the red thread—foremost, it can't be forced. In fact, it's better to forgo a red thread than to force one.

It requires a broad perspective and dynamic brainstorming that are critical to the ideation of a memorable red thread. I vividly recall a session that led to a brilliant red-thread idea for one of our storytelling agency clients. The client was pitching a large deal in the oil and gas sector, and after fleshing out ideas, the team came to me with an idea. The top of their list? "One of these things is not like the other." My reaction? Utter shock—followed by silence. Was a catchy tune from Sesame Street about to anchor our clients' pitch for a major business deal in oil and gas?

I was happy to learn (once my heart rate normalized) that there would be no cartoon cameos in the presentation. What emerged was one of the most brilliant and fitting red threads we've ever developed. It perfectly articulated our client's unique stance in a competitive, often homogeneous market, turning a commonality into a distinctive advantage. This serves as a potent reminder of the first principle in red-thread development: genuine creativity flourishes under freedom, not force.

A forced red thread would have used oil barrels, drilling rigs, and pipeline metaphors—the obvious imagery that every other presentation in the industry leans on. Picture slides littered with "drilling down into the data," "pipeline of opportunities," and "striking oil with our solution." The audience would have mentally checked out before the third "gushing with potential" reference. Not only would this approach have been painfully predictable, but it would have also undermined our client's core message about being unique in a commodity market. Using industry clichés to tell a story about being unique is like wearing the same uniform to stand out from the crowd.

The second caution of equal importance is the frequency of red-thread narrative, slide copy, or visuals. DaVinci said that "Simplicity is the ultimate sophistication," and who doesn't want a presentation pitch that's appreciated for its sophistication? Therefore, while the number can't be a lockdown rule, it can be yet another guideline based loosely on the 80/20 rule. **Twenty percent red thread is all an audience needs to remember your story.**

Threading Your Story Together

Using the *EQ Sandwich*™ structure to build a talk-track for a conversation simplifies monitoring the 20% usage of your red-thread theme, as you're only dealing with a single medium—speaking. This direct control makes it straightforward to keep track of how much you're focusing on the theme. In contrast, creating a video or presentation introduces complexity because the audience engages with the red thread through multiple sensory channels and mediums, such as audio, text, and visuals. This multifaceted approach can make it more challenging to gauge and control the extent to which the red thread permeates the content. For presentation slides or video formats, your clever theme can manifest itself in the following ways:

> **Twenty percent red thread is all an audience needs to remember your story.**

- Through the narrative talk-track,
- With words on the slides or screen, and
- Via visual imagery displayed on the slides or screen.

When a presenter or videographer uses a combination of talk, words, and visuals on a single slide, it can easily push the content over the 20% red-thread usage threshold. For instance, employing all three elements extensively on just 6 out of 20 slides can lead to an overload.

To mitigate this risk, it is beneficial to apply the *spacing effect*, a well-documented cognitive phenomenon. This effect suggests that spreading certain information across a presentation rather than concentrating it densely enhances learning and retention. By interleaving different themes or ideas across the presentation, the content remains engaging and fresh, continually recapturing the audience's attention.

Prominent cognitive psychologist Robert Bjork emphasizes that spacing out information presents a beneficial challenge to learners. It prompts them to recall previously learned material, thus strengthening memory retention[26]. In the following examples, we demonstrate practical applications of the *spacing effect* in slide presentations, showing effective ways to distribute content to maximize audience engagement and learning:

Red-Thread Application in Narrative Talk-Track Only

Figure 12.2: Weave your story through words alone, speaking to the red thread of auto racing, keeping your audience connected with a narrative that resonates and sticks.

---

[26] Bjork, Robert A., "Memory and Meta-memory Considerations in the Training of Human Beings," in *Metacognition: Knowing About Knowing*, ed. Janet Metcalfe and Arthur Shimamura (MIT Press, 1994), 185–205.

Threading Your Story Together

Red-Thread Application with Slide Words Only

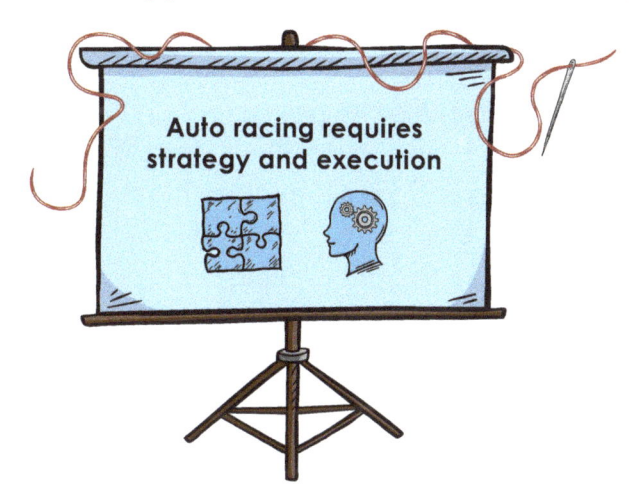

Figure 12.3: Occasionally utilize slide text that echoes the red thread of auto racing. Avoid using any verbal explanations or images directly related to the red thread. Instead, maintain standard visuals unrelated to the theme to subtly reinforce the narrative through the power of words alone.

Red-Thread Application with Imagery & Slide Words Only

Figure 12.4: Integrate visuals and text to reinforce your red thread of auto racing, ensuring your message is not just seen, but felt, by weaving an interesting and memorable story.

Story: The Currency of Influence

By demonstrating these principles through approximately 14% of our red-thread racing-analogy language in this section, we've shown how *spacing effect* integrates key themes to enhance message memorability and portability. This measured approach transforms concepts into stories that audiences can easily recall and share. While we've explored various applications of the red thread, balance is crucial—enough to keep the narrative engaging without becoming overwrought or, as Gen Z might say, "a bit cringy." Think of it as finessing the throttle—maintaining momentum without turning your Grand Prix story into a cheese parade. This deliberate balance ensures your story resonates, races through minds, and crosses the finish line as a compelling, shareable experience. Such strategic application not only reinforces your credibility but demonstrates how theory translates into practice.

From Launchpad to Landing

With these principles of red-thread placement established, let's see them in action through the *Apollo 13* journey. This practical example shows how to weave your theme throughout a presentation while maintaining the perfect balance:

Emotional Alignment — SLIDES 1–5, ABOUT THEM

Slide 1—About Them

The decision-maker's job is challenging but straightforward: orbit, land on the moon, and return home safely.

Avoid the temptation to start with the "about us" slide at the beginning. The audience has little reason to care yet. Instead, establish an emotional connection with your audience by demonstrating that you understand the situation. It could be as simple as job responsibilities or market trends in a business context.

Slide 2—Uh-Oh ...

Houston, we have a problem. The ship is running low on oxygen and doesn't have a backup system.

The second slide is where we bring in the key difficulties they face. These are a few critical challenges you've chosen because you quickly demonstrate that you understand the headaches they experience.

Slide 3—So What?

It only takes minutes for cerebral hypoxia to become fatal.

This is the most critical introduction slide and the one that is most often skipped. We may assume it's obvious why the stakes are high, but if you want to trigger their emotions, you need to clarify why their headaches might escalate into something worse because you will later show a legitimate, differentiating value proposition that solves them.

Slide 4—Ah-Ha!

You need a solution that allows you to produce additional oxygen using only the components you already have on board.

Story: The Currency of Influence

Now that you have their blood pressure up, you can start showing them a path through the minefield—identifying key actions they need to seize opportunities and mitigate the risks you just presented. Be careful, though, keep this pathway generic and market-specific—but not your company sales pitch. Get them to just embrace what any suitable solution may look like.

Slide 5—About Us

This will be our finest hour. Here is our solution that will meet your needs.

Now—when the audience cares—is the time to talk about your company, especially about what is important to them. From here on out, they are fully aware of their stake in what you have to say and will be listening carefully.

12
Meaning with Clarity

SLIDES 6–12
MIDDLE SLIDES

Slides 6–12—Middle Slides

It's solution time. Put a square peg in a round hole.

The middle slides are where you can place the facts and intellectual points of your value solution because they will be in the context of the

Threading Your Story Together

story you started. You must not over-index on solutions for the sake of appearing smart but make certain the solutions you present are clearly connected to the severe pains you addressed in the "So What?" slide.

You can also help keep the emotive connection progressing by eschewing IQ titles—that miss an opportunity to connect because they barely clarify the topic—for EQ headlines that immediately force the audience to undergo emotional relevance to them.

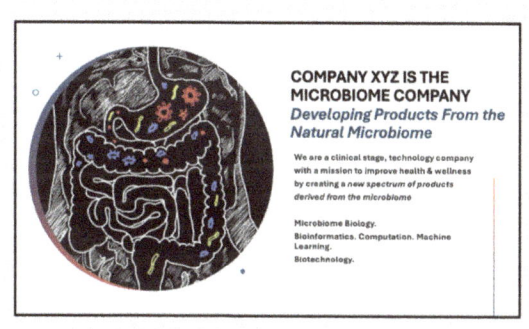

Figure 12.5: Many slides follow this format and illustrate the communication error of missing the relevance for the audience.

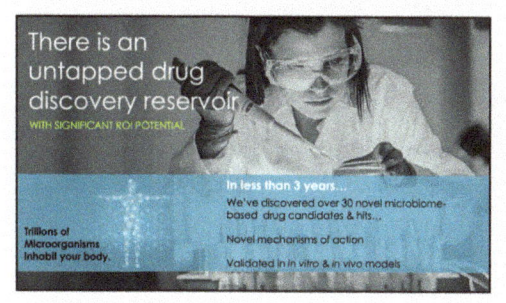

Figure 12.6: Just like your EQ slides in the first part of the sandwich, your IQ slides in the middle of the sandwich still require a dose of emotional relevance.

125

As shown in Figure 12.6, notice how the EQ is supported by straightforward validation and credentialing metrics. The slide demonstrates this by leading with an emotionally engaging headline about untapped potential, followed by concrete data: "In less than 3 years, we've discovered over 30 novel microbiome-based drug candidates." This two-part structure—emotional connection first, intellectual validation second—creates a pathway that resonates with humans. And remember the goal in this IQ section is not for you to feel smart, but to make your audience feel that way.

EQ
Story

SLIDES 13–16
RED THREAD

Slide 13—Demonstrate Your Vulnerability

It's like trying to drive a toaster through a car wash.

The astronaut confessed to mission control that he was afraid to flip on a switch in the command module. His willingness to demonstrate vulnerability bought him credibility with mission control. Leaders who practice honest vulnerability experience increased trust from others.[27] You just finished offering a host of perfect solutions. But

---

[27] Meyer, Frauke, Deidre M. LeFevre, Viviane M. J. Robinson, "How Leaders Communicate Their Vulnerability," Emerald Insight, *International Journal of Education Management* 31, no. 2 (2017): 221–235.

everybody knows nothing is perfect. As a business partner once told me, this concept of value imperfection was recognized as early as the 15th century in the Japanese philosophy of wabi-sabi: Embrace vulnerability and find beauty in life's flaws.

Slide 14—Pump the Brakes on Selling Utopia and Ask Them to Speak

We're not in the clear yet, we calculated for toting 300 pounds of moon rocks.

As humans, the audience expects the end is coming, just like the moviegoers believed a happy ending was imminent as the astronauts approached Earth. But there was more unfolding that made this last act compelling. Concerning persuasion, particularly in closing a deal, it's critical to tailor your approach based on the specific context of the engagement with your prospect. Two common scenarios often arise:

Scenario #1, Competitive Bid: Here, the prospect has initiated a Request for Proposal (RFP) and is actively evaluating options from multiple competitors. Your challenge is to distinguish your solution as not only viable but the best fit for their needs.

Scenario #2, Direct Engagement: In this case, the prospect has not explicitly sought solutions, but you've secured their attention through persistence and strategic outreach. The prospect is less committed and might consider maintaining the status quo, making your task to create a sense of urgency and highlight the potential costs of inaction.

For each scenario, the strategy involves framing questions even though they expect a silver-tongued flourish of words. The questions must provoke thoughtful consideration of the future implications of their decision:

Scenario #1: When dealing with a competitive bid, ask, "As you weigh your decision, how do you envision the chosen solution advancing your goals and addressing the aforementioned key challenges over the next 2 to 5 years?" This question encourages the prospect to think critically about the long-term benefits of your solution relative to their strategic objectives.

Scenario #2: If the engagement is more direct and there's no competitive bid, consider posing the question, "What will doing nothing look like in 2, 5, or 10 years?" The intent is to stir consideration of the risks and missed opportunities by opting for no action.

In both scenarios, the goal is to shift the prospect's perspective, making them reconsider their current position by tapping into their emotions and highlighting the future stakes involved. This approach not only addresses the immediate need but also positions your solution as the ethical and logical choice.

Slide 15—Now Is the Time to Pitch

We've never lost an American in space. Failure is not an option!

Bring back the high-level differentiating value proposition from the "About Us" slide. Say the same thing slightly differently, but don't lose the meaning. *Tell them the value this brings to their situation—not your solution.*

Scenario #1: For the competitive bid opportunity, this is the slide you end on. Keep it on-screen if you are in-person, and if you are virtual, stop sharing when done and get your face front and center. Resist the temptation to finish with a summary or recapping why you are great; instead, keep your focus squarely fixed on their situation, meeting their objectives, and overcoming challenges.

Scenario #2: For the direct engagement, you have one more closing slide.

Slide 16—Multiple Paths to Mission Success

(Scenario #2 only)

When will we be going back to the moon, and who will that be?

This final slide helps you navigate beyond mere presentation closure—it prepares you and your audience for the next steps. Offering multiple calls to action can empower your audience to make a decision that resonates with their current position. While a single call to action might lead to inaction, presenting two or three options can cater to varying readiness levels among your audience, enhancing the likelihood of advancement.

If you've read just the bold headlines in the preceding example, you've just experienced the high-level structure of a story arc like the one in the movie *Apollo 13*. Where the challenge of holding attention is paramount, the good news is that we can apply this principle in our business applications because we are the same humans wired for narratives that latch onto stories that weave emotional engagement with logical arguments. This is where the *EQ Sandwich*™ comes into play. It's not just a tool, but a transformative approach to business storytelling. Just as bread holds a sandwich together, a well-structured narrative holds the attention and interest of your audience, ensuring your message is relevant and meaningful.

Synthesizing Persuasion

Let's be clear: as businesspeople, we use storytelling to ethically persuade our audience. We've shared with you the challenges your audience faces and the structure behind successful stories; now it's time to bring it all together by revisiting the concept of *persuasion*. Modern society has made this word feel disreputable, even though it isn't. Nearly 20 centuries ago, it was properly defined. Whatever your beliefs, most can agree that the Holy Bible offers countless tidbits of wisdom sprinkled throughout our daily language; "A drop in the bucket" (Is 40:15), "Writing is on the wall" (Dan 5), "A leopard cannot change his spots" (Jer 13). In the New Testament, the author James defines types of wisdom we can receive and need to be aware of:

1. Earthly Wisdom—drives competition, jealousy, and disorder
2. Divine Wisdom—Pure, full of God's mercy and peace
3. Compliant Wisdom: Ready to listen, open to persuasion

In this last category, Compliant Wisdom, we encounter *persuasion* in its noblest form. This isn't about strong-arming opinions; it's about opening ears and minds. Ready to listen, eager to understand, and willing to apply what makes sense—this is the essence of ethical persuasion. In an ideal world, we wouldn't need to precede *persuasion* with "ethical" because true persuasion isn't inherently good or bad—it's the practitioners who tilt the scale. Yet, when we promote methods like the *Neuroscience of Persuasion*^{SM}, it is crucial to highlight responsible use of this framework to ensure it doesn't fall into the hands of users who have unethical intentions.

Synthesizing persuasive arguments is a high-stakes approach for business deals, which is why we have researched and worked diligently over the years to build the *Neuroscience of Persuasion*^{SM}. We had to go beyond the pixie-dust solutions that a quick internet search would reveal, a 3-minute article read that magically converts your content into an awesome story.

With a solid ethical foundation, we've crafted a communication model for presenting, for important discussions, or for video production, which is grounded in early philosophical insights on how we best influence others. We've enhanced this framework with science-backed research on the primacy of EQ-based communication that guides us toward the most advantageous decisions, understanding how we best receive and process information. By adopting the ancient writers' technique of *Inclusio* to engage audiences effectively, we applied a robust structure to the content. Additionally, we wove in the unifying

Threading Your Story Together

concept of the red thread, making the content both interesting and memorable. These foundational elements, which we have detailed for you, form the core of our *Neuroscience of Persuasion*^{SM}:

ARISTOTLE'S
PERSUASION FORMULA

Modern Science
Validation & EQ Primacy

Neuroscience of Persuasion™

A biological framework for successful presentations

Writing Mechanism, *Inclusio*

Red Thread
Connecting Your Story

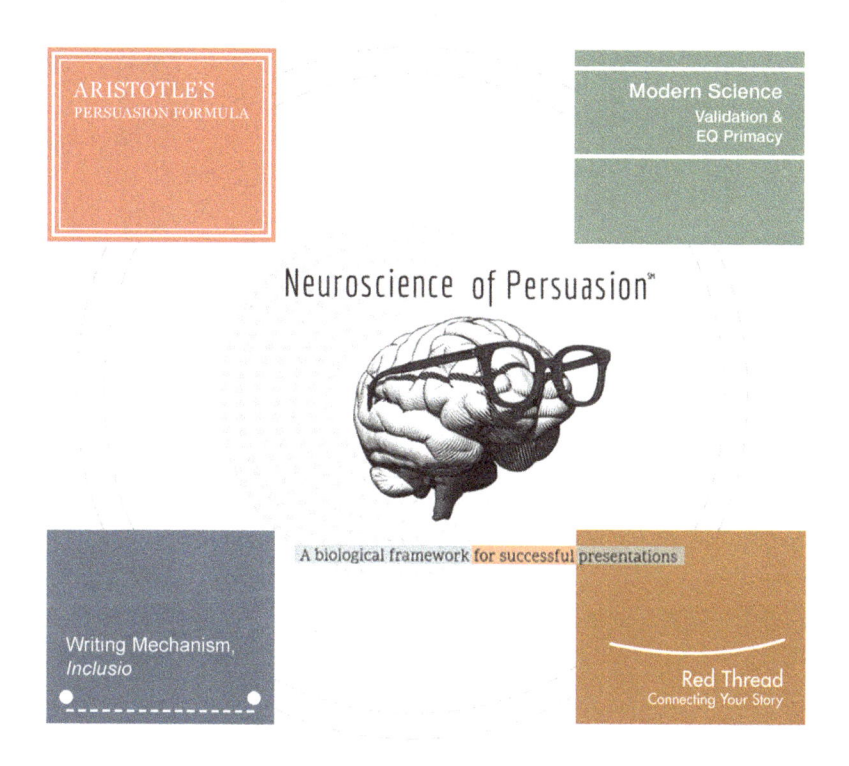

Figure 12.7: The communication model for the *Neuroscience of Persuasion*^{SM} framework blends ancient persuasion principles, modern science on emotional intelligence, the technique of *Inclusio* for engaging content, and the red thread for coherence.

Storytelling extends beyond mere language—it engages multiple senses, whether it's the ambiance of an oral tale or the visuals in a presentation. Ignoring our human biology, psychology, and the environment when trying to put our best foot forward through communication is unwise if you want to increase the probability of achieving desired ethical outcomes. Do yourself a favor and **invest as much time in your story as you do in your solution.** Using our proven framework, validated in thousands of presentation situations,

131

Story: The Currency of Influence

will make you more efficient and increase positive outcomes. However, even if you don't use our suggested framework, focusing on your story equal to or greater than your solution will still put you ahead.

Invest as much time in your story as you do in your solution.

13

Following Our Own Recipe

Guess How This Book
Is Structured ...

Story: The Currency of Influence

You know how a celebrity chef looks at the camera with that twinkle in their eye as they reveal their ingredients, including that special spice no one expected? That's exactly what we're about to do. I'm about to offer what very few authors can. This entire book hasn't just been teaching you about story structure—it's been demonstrating it. Think about your journey through these pages. We began by connecting with your world, your challenges, your desire to influence others. Then we built a foundation of science and structure. Now we're bringing it all together to empower your action.

Sound familiar?

The Structure of THIS Book

The EQ Sandwich™

CLOSING EQ (Chapters 13–15)

— Following Our Own Recipe
— Winning Your World
— Your World Tomorrow

MIDDLE IQ (Chapters 10–12)

— The Science of Story
— The *EQ Sandwich™*
— Threading Your Story

OPENING EQ (Chapters 1–9)

— Your World Today
— Everybody's a Storyteller
— Aristotle Meets (Rocket) Science

Building the structure of a book about *story*, was as easy as laying out a 15-slide deck following the *Neuroscience of Persuasion*[SM] framework.

Following Our Own Recipe

Just as we've taught you about thematic elements, we've woven our own red threads throughout this book to the level of 14.7%, well below the recommended 20% threshold. This serves as a good example of "less is more," which makes the content more memorable.

3.3%

GOLF THEME (22 instances)
- "like a wide-open fairway in golf"
- "Strategically placed markers on a golf course"
- "the final 72nd hole of a golf tournament"

7.4%

RACING THEME (50 instances)
- "when adjusting your Formula 1 race car"
- "the final lap of a Formula 1 race"
- "let's pull the engine cover off the race car"

4.0%

SPACE EXPLORATION (27 instances)
- "a storyline about a rocket ship trip to the moon"
- "the awe-inspiring Saturn V rocket"
- "even a complex rocket ship has …"

In revealing our own recipe, we've gone beyond teaching to demonstrating. This book embodies every principle we've shared: from the *EQ Sandwich*™ structure organizing our chapters to the carefully measured red threads weaving through our narrative. We began with your world, advanced through scientific foundation, and now conclude with clear action steps that should reignite those emotions.

Like the *Apollo 13* mission, this journey required precise engineering behind the scenes. Yet the result appears as natural as a well-crafted story should. By pulling back the curtain on our own process, we've shown that these principles don't just work in theory—they work whether you're crafting a 15-slide deck or, in our case, a complete book about the art of storytelling itself.

Remember: the best stories don't just tell—they show. And that's exactly what we've done here.

135

14

Winning Your World

Synthesize Story

Welcome to Your World

There has been a significant shift in the business world since the boomer generation dominated the landscape. According to data, around 56.1 million baby boomers were in the workforce in 2010.[28] By 2023, this number has decreased because of retirements and aging. As of recent data, the number of Baby Boomers in the workforce has fallen to approximately 33 million[29] and has been supplemented by the subsequent generations, especially Millennials and Generation Z. They use an increasing rate of technology and applications that are native to them. Somewhere in the early 2000s, I can recall my children having homework assignments that required a completed presentation, including visuals. This early adoption of presentation tools in education was a clear indicator of how presentation software would become fundamental to business communication.

Fast forward to today's world. Technology and communication tools like *PowerPoint* have become quite popular among the age group 16 to 24 years, with almost half of them (48%) using it regularly, compared to only around 28% usage among individuals aged 55 and above[30]. This notable contrast in usage patterns suggests younger people not only have a comfort level with such software but are also likely to continue incorporating it into both their personal and professional spheres as they grow older. As these younger individuals progress in their careers and professions, presentation software will become even more deeply embedded in business communications.

As stated by Acuity Training (UK), there has been an increase in search queries related to "PowerPoint" and "Google Slides," with

---

[28] Fry, Richard, "Millennials Are the Largest Generation in the U.S. Labor Force," Pew Research Center, April 11, 2018, www.pewresearch.org/fact-tank/2018/04/11/millennials-largest-generation-us-labor-force.

[29] "Labor Force Statistics," United States Census Bureau, Census.gov, www.census.gov/data/tables/time-series/demo/popest/2020s-counties-total.html.

[30] "PowerPoint Statistics: Usage & Market Share in 2023," Acuity Training, April 19 2023, www.acuitytraining.co.uk/news-tips/powerpoint-statistics/.

numbers soaring from 52 million in 2016 to a staggering 103 million in 2022. This surge in search activity highlights the growing importance of presentation tools, particularly because of the exposure of younger generations to such software. With integrating presentation software into processes becoming increasingly common, it is expected that its usage will become more widespread across industries.

You Can't Escape

Everyone now must give presentations; therefore, storytelling becomes the currency of success. As the future becomes increasingly less about solutions—especially where technology can accelerate quickly in competitive environments—then you, and how well you can articulate a compelling and memorable story, will matter. Imagine two identically prepared Formula 1 race cars—one driven by a world champion the other by the 20th-place driver on the grid. Who are you betting on to deliver results? In this age of artificial intelligence, when anyone can click their return key and get a presentation, who's going to win? The one who understands the fundamentals of a story or the one who relies on the technological know-how and the fastest path to presentation.

> Everyone now must give presentations; therefore, storytelling becomes the currency of success.

Go Ahead, Keep My Attention

The world is repeatedly amplifying this message today. *Show me* why your idea, solution, or business is worthy without losing my attention. In the business of holding attention, there's no industry more focused on the shifts in human nature than those who produce movies. The

Story: The Currency of Influence

British film scholar Barry Salt collected data from over 15,000 movies dating from 1910 through 2014. His finding was that film-shot lengths have shrunk from 12 seconds in 1930 to 2.5 seconds in 2014.[31]

Figure 14.1: No industry adapts better to human tendencies than the movie industry, where our attention spans require shorter film-shot lengths.

With substantial usage among younger generations, which suggests a growing trend in utilizing video presentations and digital content across both personal and professional contexts, YouTube has captured the mindshare of 2.49 billion monthly active users.[32] That's nearly 10 times more than Netflix! Even at that scope and volume, they realized the demand for easier consumption when several other social applications used shorter video clips. Today, the platform offers a category called *shorts,* which are created specifically for our shorter attention

---

31 Miller, Greg, "Data from a Century of Cinema Reveals How Movies Have Evolved," Wired, *Condé Nast*, 24 Sept. 2014, https://www.wired.com/2014/09/cinema-is-evolving/.
32 Singh, Shubham, "How Many People Use YouTube 2024." Demandsage, November 14, 2024, https://www.demandsage.com/youtube-stats/.

spans by viewing short-form video content, usually 60 seconds or less. This informs us that:

- Concise communication is crucial
- Visual and EQ-based content creates engagement
- Innovative presentation methods hold attention
- Formats should be simple and memorable
- The narrative should be the focus

These points highlight the importance of storytelling in the modern business landscape. As attention spans shrink, the ability to convey important information quickly and memorably becomes crucial. Adopting this new currency of success leverages the trends observed in short-form content adopted by social media platforms and, if applied to presentation, opportunities can significantly enhance the effectiveness of business storytelling.

15

Your World Tomorrow

The Currency of Success

Story: The Currency of Influence

Your Prospects Will Thank You

You've made it through STORY—*The Currency of Influence*. No small feat, considering we've asked your brain to juggle cognitive load, neurobiology, and EQ all at once. Hopefully, you're now seeing how these elements are the key benefit for today's currency of influence.

Here's the million-dollar question to ask yourself: "Is there an emotional connection in every piece of communication we send to our prospects?" Without that emotional spark, not only do you miss the opportunity to connect, but you also make it unnecessarily difficult for your client to act on the value of your offering. So, go forth and sprinkle those emotional breadcrumbs in your communication. Your prospects' brains will thank you, even if they don't know why.

Knowing Their Emotional Landscape

Remember the importance of focusing on gaining an EQ audience snapshot. Skipping that step leads to wasted time glorifying solutions no one asked for. It's like obsessing about how to pound your drives in golf farther when it's your short game—putting—that sucks and keeps you from lowering your score. Dealmakers and content owners sometimes find themselves caught in a similar trap: focusing on amplifying their own innovative service model or delivery approach while neglecting the nuances of their client's pain points and decision-making criteria.

By shifting your perspective to deeply understand your audience's emotional landscape, you simplify content development. By understanding routine headaches that they face, and how some of those can escalate into career defining migraines, you move away from overselling features and instead squarely focus using newfound language on what matters: *their* situation. This approach doesn't just get you to the finish line—it transforms your ability to connect with decision-makers, gaining insights that elevate your value solution beyond just another option in the market. Imagine your deal team being able to allocate resources more effectively. Who wants more time to focus on their other responsibilities? Sign me up!

By going through this process, you achieve more than just an end goal; this becomes an eye-opening experience that transforms your entire perspective on the engagement opportunity. When you shift your focus to truly understanding your audience's situation, something magical happens.

Throughout our storytelling agency's history, client praise poured in after every session where we developed an EQ Snapshot of an audience. Many participants realized that the price of our service was justified by the insights gained from this audience exploration alone. They discovered an inordinate amount of focus on their own company's solution, neglecting what truly mattered—their audience's needs. These "lightbulb moments" have been some of the most fulfilling experiences in our nearly two-decade journey serving global clients. Honestly, witnessing these epiphanies makes all the hard work worthwhile!

With your audience-centric approach in place, you've automatically achieved story distillation. Think of it as the last lap of a Formula 1 race—you've navigated the tricky corners, you're positioned to win, now it's all about precision and focus. Distillation strips your message to its essence, like hitting the perfect apex in a high-speed corner, or sinking a crucial putt on the 72nd hole of a golf tournament.

When you achieve this level of distillation, something magical happens. Your audience doesn't just understand your story—they own it. They can repeat it without you, scaling its impact beyond the room. This is why the *EQ Sandwich*[TM] structure lives in your head, not your deck. True storytelling mastery isn't about perfect slides—it's about embodying your message until it becomes part of who you are.

You Are the Deck

With this newfound mastery, you're equipped to execute a better story that is both persuasive and emotionally resonant with your audience. The framework of the *Neuroscience of Persuasion*^{SM} shows you *how* to execute a better story. It's up to you to always have the *why* in front of you, and the why is all about a more persuasive and emotional connection with your audience. Remember, storytelling isn't just a technique; it's the currency of influence. Whether we acknowledge it, we are all storytellers in today's world. The deck is just a support application.

When I said earlier that your most powerful asset is you, not your presentation, I meant it literally. A friend of mine once illustrated this perfectly. When a board of directors asked him to present without a deck, his response was, *"I am the* [#!% expletive] *deck, baby!"*

Now go, be the deck.

Acknowledgments

I'm no different from most people in that each of us has limited origination of ideas. We have a few here and there, but certainly not enough to pen a book. But what I have been fortunate with is an ability to pull together brilliant insights from those more talented than I and to spin those into something that hopefully makes sense. That's what you'll find in this book—a carefully sewn patchwork of wisdom from an incredible group of people. Without their influence, none of this would be possible.

Sure, I've included citations for the obvious sources. But this book is also a testament to the countless others who have shaped my career and life. To my business peers, I've shamelessly borrowed more from you than you probably realize—and certainly more than I could ever repay. I won't mention last names here, so if you have a unique first name, congratulations, you're in. To the rest of you ... well, you know who you are: Jeff, Cheyenne, Adam, Mike, Jim, Emil, Joan, Hans, Jennifer, Prashant, Reid, Dennis, Chris, Gene, Julie, Tim, James, Jens, Mark, Tina, John, Peter, Vadim, Colby, Kevin, Franz, Diane, Mara, Tony, Tiffani, Thomas, Kathryn, Donna, Daniel, Betsy, Kraig, Ted, Daniel, Richard, Gisselle, Omar, Debbie, Danielle, Todd, Greg, and Engela.

And finally, to you, the reader. A recipe is just words on a page until someone steps into the kitchen. My suggestion is for you to bring your own ingredients to this conversation about story. I hope that you'll take these collective insights, add your unique flavors, and cook up something remarkable.

Story: The Currency of Influence

A Triple-Quad of Espresso Shots of Wisdom

Intense flavored ideas to boost your storytelling prowess

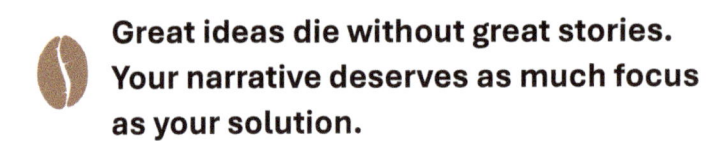

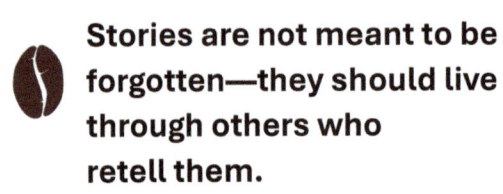

- **Great ideas die without great stories. Your narrative deserves as much focus as your solution.**

- **Algorithms don't make decisions; humans do.**

- **Stories are not meant to be forgotten—they should live through others who retell them.**

(Aesop's Tortoise and the Hare)

- When less than half your prep time focuses on your audience, you're not telling their story—you're just selling your capabilities.

- When we only show the good, we leave our skeptical client audience to imagine the bad.

- Trust deepens when your narrative honestly weaves together both victories and challenges.

- Emotions anchor memories—making them last longer and stay clearer than neutral events.

- Our brains resist action when logic stands alone.

- When audiences wrestle with granular intricacies they've lost sight of your larger story.

- When a fact is wrapped in a story, it is 7 to 10 times more memorable.

- Invest as much time in your story as you do in your solution.

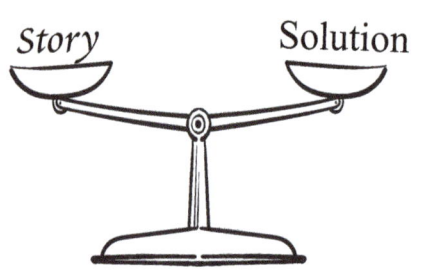

- Everyone now must give presentations; therefore storytelling becomes the currency of success.